"A commentary of commentaries or

EDWARD P. MILLER, DIR

MW00451711

"Read this book, learn again why yo
and have that love rekindled again!"

TONY DALE, FOUNDER, HOUSE 2 HOUSE; CHAIRMAN, THE KARIS GROUP

"Oh, I am enjoying the devotional book tremendously! In fact I am devouring it!
Thank you again for this extraordinary gift!"

CHRISSIE SHAHEEN, THE TENT, INC., ISRAEL

"Full of fire and life and passion and eternal truth! It drew me to Him—over and
over again."—

JAN WINTERBURN, FEDEX, TENNESSEE

"The Lord used this book to bring me back into His loving arms in a fresh and
restorative way. I want to start reading it all over again!"

LORI DREXLER, FIRST FRUIT, INC.

"I have never read a more beautiful commentary and devotional on the Song of
Solomon. It will bless many all over the world."

LAZARUS YEGHNAZAR, 222 MINISTRIES

"From the time I began reading His Desire Is for Me, I have been blessed out of
my socks! I think you wrote the book just for me! Now that I have finished, I am
having withdrawal pains!"

BETTY HAWKINS, INTERCESSOR MINISTRY, CALIFORNIA

"Very moving!"

LISA LODEN, NAZARETH EVANGELICAL THEOLOGICAL SEMINARY

"It is one thing to write a book, another to write well; it is one thing to write well,
but much rarer to write worthy content . . . and even rarer to write content and be
readable. The author has done all this in His Desire Is for Me. Perhaps we have
here a greater rarity still, the birth of a good author!"

GENE EDWARDS, AUTHOR, *TALE OF THREE KINGS*,
THE DIVINE ROMANCE, AND OTHER TITLES

"You put into words something that is inexpressible."

MIKE KUSESKE, CHRISTIAN ARTIST, FLORIDA

"To me, the Song of Songs has always been the most delicious book of the Bible. Even as a guy, I've never had a problem putting myself in the Shulammite's sandals and delighting in its rich intimacies. Thank you, Bob Emery, for giving us a fresh way of enjoying this timeless story and deepening our yearning to make it our own."

RON BRACKIN, N.Y. TIMES BESTSELLING AUTHOR OF SON OF HAMAS

"Everything I have ever read on the Song of Songs is heavy and dry. Your book flows beautifully. It unlocks the mysteries in the Song of Songs in a beautiful and poetic style that touches the heart of its reader deeply."

GEORGES HOUSSNEY, PRESIDENT HORIZONS INTERNATIONAL

"Many people know and understand very little about Song of Songs. In His Desire is For Me, I found a new level of love and spiritual intimacy with Christ described so beautifully. If you know me well, you know that I don't often recommend books. However, this is one I strongly recommend!"

ISIK ABLA, CHRISTIAN SATELLITE TV HOST: LIGHT FOR THE HEART, TURKEY

"I started reading His Desire Is for Me a couple weeks ago and every single reading has touched me in a profound way. It's like the Lord is speaking these things directly to me knowing the exact season I'm in and what I need to hear. If writing this book was for only one person, that one person was me!"

JULIE BERNSTEIN, SINGER-SONGWRITER

"Stunningly written. Much in the same way Jesus taught, Bob Emery teaches of God's love for each of us through his beautiful storyline, gentle style and vibrant visual images. I became so enthralled with the story I could smell the combination dust and scented oils when the King's chariot rolled by, feel Jerusalem's sun on my face, and I could also feel my desire to be closer to Him welling up inside my heart."

JACK BISHOP, KENTUCKY

"Congratulations on creating a masterpiece on one of the most difficult books of the Bible!"

LEVENT KINRAN, TURKEY

"I cannot express how much this book has meant to me. Every chapter is as if completing a picture of my life with Him, each day gives more sense to what I have been through."

YOLI LOZA, MISSIONARY, PERU

HIS DESIRE IS FOR ME:

THE STORY OF SOLOMON AND THE SHULAMMITE

A 30-DAY DEVOTIONAL AND COMMENTARY ON THE SONG OF SONGS

BOB EMERY

BENCH PRESS PUBLISHING
"Be strong in the Lord"

HIS DESIRE IS FOR ME

© 2011 Bob Emery

Scripture taken from the *New American Standard Bible*, © Copyright 1960, 1962, 1963, 1968, 1971, 1972, 1973, 1975, 1977, 1995 by The Lockman Foundation. Used by permission.

The poem "Let Us Contemplate the Grapevine" by Watchman Nee is used by permission, © Living Stream Ministry.

Illustrations by Tim Irvin
Tirvin4@triad.rr.com

Published by
BenchPress Publishing
P.O. Box 5846
Charlottesville, VA 22905

www.BobEmeryBooks.com

ISBN 978-0-9669747-2-0

Printed in the USA

Cover design by Robin Black, Blackbird Designs

Dedication

To all those who love the Lord and would desire to be his Shulammite.

Table of Contents

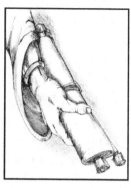

The Song of Songs, Which Is Solomon's

It was almost dusk when the young woman arrived at the private residence of Ahijah, King Solomon's personal secretary. She knocked on the door. As she waited for an answer, she smelled the delightful fragrance from the two flowering jasmine plants in large jars standing in the entryway. Finally, a youthful, barefoot servant boy opened the door.

"I would like to see Ahijah," she told the boy. "I know that he is not expecting me, but it will take only a minute."

"What is your name?" he asked.

"Tell him that Shirel is here to see him."

"Who are you, and what family are you from?" he inquired.

"It will be enough to tell him that Shirel wishes to see him. He will know who I am."

The boy turned abruptly and disappeared down a corridor until the patter of his feet could be heard no more. Several minutes later a slender, older man with a wrinkly face, long, stringy gray hair, and a cropped gray beard appeared in the doorway.

"Well, if it isn't Shirel!" he said with a slight chuckle. "It has been a long time since I have seen you. What brings you to Jerusalem and here to my house this night?"

"Greetings, Ahijah," she replied. "It is good to see you again. My husband and I arrived only yesterday in Jerusalem. I knew that it would be too difficult to see you at the palace during the day, so I came this night hoping to find you at home. Please forgive me for not making an appointment."

"You have done no harm," the old man said. "What is your purpose for this visit?"

"We have come to offer our sacrifice for the Passover in four days and then stay for the Feast of Weeks three days later to offer our firstfruits. My husband's parents are elderly and in poor health, so we must return to our home immediately following the celebration. But while we are here, I want very much to see the king. My purpose in coming to your home this evening was to see if you might schedule a time for us to do so."

Ahijah frowned. "With the Passover upon us, the city swelling with pilgrims and worshipers, and the long list of visitors seeking audience with the king—it will be nearly impossible with such short notice. You know that the king is a very, very busy man."

"I know that he is," she responded, her tone pleading. "But promise me just this. Promise that you will let him know that I am here. That is all. The rest I will leave in God's hands."

"Very well, Shirel," the old man conceded. "That much I can do. I wish you well. Shalom, and good night."

The following morning, in his customary manner, Ahijah sat with the king to discuss his personal calendar—doing his best to ignore the ruler's stormy mood.

"Your schedule is a rather full one today," he said. "The sailors sent by Hiram of Tyre, bearing gold and precious stones from Ophir, have arrived. They wish to see you. The merchants you dispatched to Egypt and Kue to purchase horses have returned and have been waiting for days here in Jerusalem to give you a report. Ben-hur, your deputy from the hill country of Ephraim, is here to see you as well."

"Is there anyone else?" the king barked.

"Yes, there are others," replied Ahijah. "The line is long. There are a few other dignitaries, some of whom you know, others whom you have never met. Some of them have been waiting for weeks—even months—to see you. I could fit one or two into your schedule—they could be here within the hour. And then there is Shirel."

"Shirel? She is here? When did she arrive? Did she come alone?" King Solomon sat up straighter in his chair, almost as one who had been aroused from a deep sleep by good news.

"Yes, she is here. She arrived in Jerusalem two days ago with her husband and came to me last night. She said she wanted to see you."

"Bring her and her husband to me at once," said the king. "And clear my schedule of all other appointments. This day belongs to them."

"But, my king, these others have been expecting—"

"Enough!" Solomon said, raising his voice. "Bring her to me now!"

Ahijah excused himself. Summoning one of his attendants, he gave instructions to go quickly to Shirel and her husband. "Bring them to the side chamber off the throne room, where the king will meet with them in private," he told the attendant.

Later that morning, the attendant escorted the couple to the chamber door. The young woman was in her early thirties. She had long, dark hair and was well proportioned and modestly dressed. Her husband was slightly older, tall, with a light brown complexion and a short beard. He appeared somewhat nervous, his palms sweating, and awed by the splendor of the palace.

"The king is inside and waiting for you," the attendant said as he pushed open the thick cedar door. "You may go on in."

The couple entered the spacious room. The king was sitting in a large, comfortable chair decorated with an embroidered fabric made of a deep, rich blue material and upheld on legs of ivory. Shirel smiled and bowed before the king, as did her husband. Interrupting her bow and the protocol, the king rose hastily from his seat, making quick strides across the room to meet her. He wrapped his arms around her, and the two embraced. Solomon held her tightly as he kissed her repeatedly on the cheek. Standing back from her, his eyes moist with tears, he said, "Shirel, it is so good to see you! You cannot imagine what a beam of sunshine you brought into the cloudy darkness of this man's life when I heard that you were here. You look wonderful—both of you do."

"I am so happy to see you, too, my king," Shirel said with a gleaming smile.

"It has been nearly ten years," Solomon said. "To what do I attribute the privilege of this visit?"

She nodded. "My husband and I have come to Jerusalem to offer sacrifice to the God of Israel and to celebrate the Passover. I have also had a longing in my heart of late to see you and learn how you are doing. But I must admit, there is another reason I have come. And perhaps, this is the deepest motive for my visit. It has been such a long time since I have seen the Shulammite. I was beginning to forget her. I was hoping that you would talk to me about her, that you would tell me stories to rekindle my precious memories of her."

With tears in his eyes, the king nodded. "I understand," he said. He motioned to the comfortably cushioned chairs next to his. "Please sit down. When I heard you were here, I anticipated that our conversation would turn to my love, the Shulammite. Knowing that, I went immediately to my room to fetch something I knew would have great meaning to you. But before I share it, I must make a confession.

"Life for me these past years has been difficult. In fact, my mind is clouded with disillusionment. Your eyes have beheld the vast kingdom over which I rule, and my stockpiles of gold, silver, and every precious thing. You have seen my military might, the weaponry of my armies, and my naval fleet. You have observed the great monuments that I have ordered to be built. But frankly, Shirel, if the truth were told, all of this is vanity and chasing after the wind."

As Shirel listened with compassion in her expression, Solomon continued. "You see, in my youth I purposed to gain wisdom and knowledge, but since then I have also known madness and folly. I have built luxurious palaces; I have planted vineyards and the most elaborate gardens. I have constructed ponds and stocked them with the most exotic fish. And I have known women—maidens without number have warmed my bed. I have withheld from myself not a single desire. But I have learned that one cannot be satisfied with gold, silver, possessions, or even pleasure. I have come to disdain my life and the fruit of my labor."

"But, my king," Shirel protested, "you have been greatly used by the Almighty. You have built the temple and the palace. You have written so many proverbs and composed so many songs. They have served as a light to guide countless souls in the truth and bring joy to their hearts."

Solomon shook his head. The sadness in his face was undeniable. "Three thousand proverbs. My songs number a thousand and five. But now there are no songs left in me. The music has ceased. Still, you are right. God is good. That is the conclusion I have reached: when all has been heard, to fear God and to keep his commandments is right for every person. But at this point, as I look back on my life, I see that I have failed with what God has entrusted to me. But that is enough about me. I am not looking for your pity, and you did not come here to listen to the confessions of a king. You came to hear about the Shulammite."

With that, he reached over to a table next him. On it, beside a candle and a large alabaster vase, lay a tightly rolled scroll with a thin, black leather tie encircling it. He picked it up, paused, and looked at it momentarily before handing it to Shirel.

"Does your husband know much about her?" he inquired.

"No more than I have told him. As you know, he only knew her briefly," she said.

The king leaned over, and with the kindest, most intent look on his face, said to her husband, "My son, listen to my words. Take what I am about to say to you as words from one who has seen much in life and been given much wisdom from the Lord. Relish life with the woman whom you love all of your fleeting days which God has given to you under the sun, for this is your reward in life."

"I thank you," Shirel's husband said, "for your wise counsel."

"What is this you have given me, my king?" asked Shirel.

"Open it," replied the king.

Shirel quickly untied the thin piece of leather that kept the scroll tightly rolled up. She scanned the long, neatly penned piece of papyrus. "It is a song!" she surmised, looking back at the king.

"It is not just a song," he answered. "This is a special song."

"A love song?" she asked.

"Indeed," he said with a smile. "It is about our love… the love between me and the Shulammite. This is not her story. It is mine. It is a song about how I loved her with a love that was birthed in my heart by the very flame of God, and about how I drew her to myself. In this song, you will see how she grew in love, how she matured, and how she responded to me. I have described some of our intimate moments, but cloaked them in the garment of poetry."

"Why have you written this?" she asked, looking up from the words on the scroll.

"I did not want a drop of the sacred love that we shared to be lost. I have written with the hope that our song will be sung by all lovers, and that they will come to know the joy that I have known."

"It looks to be so personal. What would you have me do with it?" Shirel asked.

"I would like you read it."

"Here and now?" she replied.

"Yes. I want to hear the story again as well. I never tire of it."

Shirel glanced over at her husband and then back to the scroll. A sacred hush enveloped the room as the three of them sat silently together.

The king leaned his head back on the chair, folded his hands across his stomach, and closed his eyes. His mouth fashioned into a slight smile.

"Do not be in a hurry," he whispered softly. "Read it as if it were a prayer being offered at the very altar of God."

Shirel took a deep breath and exhaled. Then, slowly, she began to read.

"May he kiss me with the kisses of his mouth…"

Introduction

Interpreting the Song of Songs

The Song of Songs (or "The Song of Solomon," as it is also called) is a spiritual treasure chest buried deep within the pages of Scripture. It contains some of the most precious and intimate revelations about the love of God for his people that have ever been penned.

There are four basic ways of looking at the Song of Songs. On a purely human level, it can be seen as a book about the sacredness of human love between a man and a woman. In fact, it is one of only two books in the Bible—the other being the Book of Esther—where the word "God" never appears, with the exception of one passing reference to "the flame of the Lord" in chapter 8. It can be appreciated apart from any spiritual significance purely for its rich, romantic description of the relationship between two lovers.

But because the Song has been included in the Bible and "all Scripture is inspired by God and profitable for teaching, for reproof, for correction, for training in right-eousness; so that the man of God may be adequate, equipped for every good work" (2 Timothy 3:16), something unique from the heart of God is also revealed in its pages.

One way to view this book, then, is to see that God not only created but approves, sanctions, and even delights in the romantic, erotic encounters between the sexes, if conducted in the proper context. If you look closely, even though God's name is not mentioned, you can see that his presence is manifest in the form of an unidentified observer. Overflowing with delight, this observer encourages the lovers in their most intimate of moments, as in the passage which reads, "Eat, friends; drink and imbibe deeply, O lovers" (Song of Songs 5:1).

A second way this book has been viewed is by Jewish scholars who see it as an allegorical story about Jehovah and Israel. In the Old Testament, God is often referred to as Israel's husband: "For your husband is your Maker, whose name is the Lord of hosts; and your Redeemer is the Holy One of Israel, who is called the God of all the earth" (Isaiah 54:5).

For New Testament Christians, the Song of Songs is often interpreted as the story of Christ's love for his bride—the church.

Finally, the book can be viewed more personally, as a message of God's love for his individual saints—you and me. That is the approach taken in this book.

The Song of Songs is one of the poetic books in the Bible. Like the Psalms, it is not a book of doctrine. It is a song. Since it allows for a mystical, spiritual, and allegorical level of interpretation, it is not a book to approach intellectually and analytically, slicing and dicing it, organizing it, and putting it into neat little categories. Instead, it is a book that needs to be engaged with the heart: it is to be savored, meditated upon, and experienced. Since intimate romance with God can only be discovered individually through life-changing, personal, one-on-one encounters with him, any commentary on the Song of Songs aimed solely at the intellect, while bypassing the heart and the spirit, would have little impact on the furtherance of spiritual growth.

THE UNIQUENESS OF THIS BOOK

Two things make this commentary on the Song of Songs unique.

The first is that it has been made into a thirty-day devotional. Unlike other commentaries, this one can be used as a daily devotional which, along with prayer and meditation, will give you the opportunity to take bite-sized portions from the Song of Songs and savor their spiritual content over a period of time. In this way, the table has been set for you, in your quiet times, to have your own personal encounters with God.

The second distinctive is the fictional account of Solomon and the Shulammite that has been added based on what is known about them from the Song of Songs and from other biblical and historical references. Through their interaction and dialogue, I have attempted to put flesh and blood on the spiritual truths and principles contained in the Song.

Much of the enduring Christian literature found on bookshelves today communicate God's truth in fiction, in story form. Take, for example, John Bunyan's *Pilgrim's Progress*. It is a Christian allegory written in 1678 which has never been out of print and is considered one of the most noteworthy pieces of English literature ever written. Hannah Hurnard's *Hind's Feet on High Places* and C.S. Lewis's Chronicles of Narnia are just two more examples of allegorical fiction that has touched the hearts of generations of Christians.

There is a reason for the enduring quality of these works. Jesus, too, knew how we humans are able to best comprehend truth. He did not give lectures based on systematic theology, but he did explain to his disciples the things concerning himself in *all* the Old Testament Scriptures—including the Song of Songs (Luke 24:27). Instead of lecturing, he often spoke in parables or told stories which put human flesh on truth. In this way, he was (and still is) able to speak directly to the hearts and spirits of his followers.

In this book, each daily devotion will have a portion of Scripture, an accompanying story that interprets what is going on in that portion, and then a commentary, followed by a final thought or a prayer. I suggest that you read each day's devotion slowly. Pray over it. Meditate upon it. And allow the Lord the opportunity to speak to you.

THE AUTHOR OF THE SONG OF SONGS

The Song of Songs was written by Solomon, the son of King David. Solomon was a fount of wisdom and song and was credited with speaking three thousand proverbs and composing one thousand and five songs (1 Kings 4:29–34).

In the Proverbs, Solomon wrote about wisdom and the rewards of wisdom. He wrote about the contrast of the righteous and the wicked, and he gave advice from lessons he had learned in life. Of the one thousand and five songs Solomon wrote, there is no record or collection. Only one was saved, and appropriately, it was called "the Song of Songs," or "the best of songs." It is a song about love. Love endures. Love never fails. As it says in 1 Corinthians 13:

> Love never fails. But if there are gifts of prophecy, they will be done away; if there are tongues, they will cease; if there is knowledge, it will be done away. For we know in part and we prophesy in part; but when the perfect comes, the partial will be done away... But now faith, hope, love, abide these three; but the greatest of these is love. (1 Corinthians 13:8–9, 13)

Chronologically, Solomon probably wrote Proverbs while in the strength of his youth. During this period, we can see in his writings strength of character and the display of high moral standards. But the Bible tells us that his heart turned from the Lord, and he went after many foreign women. He took seven hundred wives and three hundred concubines, fell into idolatry, and ended up being responsible for dividing the kingdoms of Israel and Judah. Sadly, Solomon did not finish well.

The Book of Ecclesiastes was probably written when he was middle-aged. By then, Solomon had tasted everything that the world had to offer. During this period of his life, Solomon became disillusioned and came to the conclusion that everything under the sun was vanity and that he had been chasing after the wind.

As for the Song of Songs, it is difficult to say when it was written. It is highly unlikely that Solomon would have written this, the best of all love songs, during his confused middle years when he was busy accumulating so many other wives and concubines! Some suggest that it was written in his old age. After many years and much reflection, Solomon was brought back to understand the real purpose of life. That purpose is to know God and to know his love, as represented by the love Solomon was given for the Shulammite. Others believe that it was written while he was living in the light of the wisdom God had given him at a time of innocence and first love. But no one knows for sure.

If we had to choose between an earlier or a later writing, the safer bet would be that the Song of Songs was probably written earlier in Solomon's life and was a description of first love. That is the position that has been taken in this book.

WHO WAS THE MAIDEN?

Many have been curious to identify the maiden, or "the Shulammite" as she is called, in this song. Who was this mysterious woman?

When looking to the Bible, we can find specific references to only two of Solomon's seven hundred wives. Solomon's life is described in 1 Kings 2–11 and 2 Chronicles 1–9. In these passages, there are several references to one particular wife—Pharaoh's daughter. The only other wife specifically named is Naamah, the Ammonitess, mentioned in 1 Kings 14:21, who was the mother of Solomon's ill-fated son Rehoboam. Both would have been married to Solomon in his early years, around the time that he began his reign as king. Some scholars contend that the Shulammite in the Song of Songs was Pharaoh's daughter. Others disagree on the grounds that the description of the young maiden is that of a poor country shepherdess, a picture at total odds with one who grew up amidst the royalty and grandeur of Pharaoh's household.

Another speculation is that the Shulammite could have been Abishag, the beautiful young virgin who was brought to King David to keep him warm on his deathbed, but with whom he did not have sexual relations (1 Kings 1:1–5). About this time, Adonijah, David's oldest son, attempted a coup to set himself up as king even while David was still alive. But David had promised Bathsheba that Solomon would follow him and inherit the throne. Once Solomon was installed as king, Adonijah came to Bathsheba and asked her to request that Solomon give him Abishag's hand in marriage, but Solomon reacted in an extreme fashion and had his brother killed (1 Kings 2:19–25). This could have been an indication that Solomon had his eyes on this beautiful maiden as well, and that she is the Shulammite in the Song. But even this interpretation is inconclusive.

What we can confidently state, however, is that both Solomon and the maiden are Old Testament pictures, or "types," that speak to us about Christ and his relationship to his bride, the church, or to the individual believer. All types in the Old Testament have their limitations and flaws: Adam was a type of Christ (Romans 5:14), yet he sinned, resulting in the fall of the whole human race. Moses was a type of Christ (1 Corinthians 10:1–6), yet his disobedience to God's voice toward the end of his life kept him from entering the Promised Land.

To be sure, Solomon had his weaknesses and sins, but God still used him as a picture to help us understand several things. In this love song, God uses Solomon as an example of how our heavenly king woos us, wins us, and draws us to himself. The maiden is a type of us as believers, so we can learn from her example what it is like to respond to the Lord's love.

If your intellectual curiosity still demands an answer as to the Shulammite's identity, consider this: It is quite conceivable that God has deliberately withheld her identity from us. While using Adam and Eve as examples of the husband-and-wife relationship in his letter to the Ephesians, Paul concluded that "This *mystery* is great; but I am speaking with reference to Christ and the church" (Ephesians 5:32, emphasis mine). In this light, it seems fitting that God chose to leave the Shulammite's identity a mystery as well, so that she could truly be a type of the church.

In God's wisdom, the historical person, whoever she might have been—with all her faults and problems—will not get in the way and become a distraction to us. Rather, we can see the maiden of the Song of Songs as a pure example of what it looks like to grow and mature in love for the Lord. Her identity is a mystery, and so, as you read her story, it becomes much easier to believe that the maiden being written about could actually be you!

The Three Stages of Love

Possibly more than any other book in the Bible, the Song of Songs contains a message that spans the whole of Christian experience. It reveals the different stages a believer goes through on the road to spiritual maturity. As our love for the Lord grows from initial love and then increases, it finally unfolds into a mature love. The Song expresses the tender tale of a monarch and a maiden; a king and his captivating bride. It is a book that reveals the passionate, intense, and jealous love that God has for *you!*

The story has been divided into three sections corresponding to each stage of love. Each section has a particular verse which characterizes the theme of that stage of the Shulammite's love relationship with her bridegroom.

The first stage is initial love. The verse characterizing this phase is chapter 2, verse 16: "My beloved is mine, and I am his." This period of the maiden's life is one of revelation and discovery. She sees many new things about her bridegroom, but they have not yet become hers in her experience. In stage one, the maiden's emphasis is on herself.

The second stage is one of increasing love. The verse that marks this phase is chapter 6, verse 3: "I am my beloved's and my beloved is mine." During this period, the maiden learns to yield and surrender to the king and his ways. Now the emphasis is on him first and her second. As John the Baptist said of Christ, "He must increase, but I must decrease" (John 3:30).

The third stage is mature love. The distinguishing verse in this section is chapter 7, verse 10: "I am my beloved's and his desire is for me." This is the stage of rest, union, and fruitfulness. By now, the maiden has reached spiritual maturity. She has entered into a union with the king. Now it is all about him and his desire for her. All she sees is his love. She trusts him. She is comfortable with him. She has become one with him in character and purpose.

THE LESSON FROM THE SONG OF SONGS

Regardless of when the Song was written, whether it was penned during or following Solomon's composition of three thousand proverbs and over a thousand songs, and regardless of who the maiden was, the conclusion remains the same. If Solomon, the man whose wisdom surpassed all men, came to the realization that the best, the greatest thing in life is love, then what lesson can we take away from this? How should this influence the measurement by which we measure our own progress in the Christian life? What benchmarks exist for us to know that we are growing in the Lord?

Do we measure our growth in the Lord by our understanding of God's Word? Do we measure it by how many years in a row we have read through the One-Year Bible? Do we measure it by the number of Scripture verses we have memorized or by how many people we have led to Christ? All of these may be valuable—but shouldn't the true measure of growth in the Lord be gauged by how much we have come to know and understand his love for us, and by how much we have grown to love him in return?

The apostle John expressed this thought in his writings. After being a follower of Christ for nearly forty years, he wrote the following:

We have come to know *and have believed the love which God has for us.* God is love, and the one who abides in love abides in God, and God abides in him. By this, love is perfected with us, so that we may have confidence in the Day of Judgment; because as He is, so also are we in this world. There is no fear in love; but perfect love casts out fear, because fear involves punishment, and the one who fears is not perfected in love. We love because He first loved us. (1 John 4:16–19, emphasis mine)

Not only did John know that God loved him, but he had come to *believe it.* The apostle Paul expressed it in another way:

For *I am convinced* that neither death, nor life, nor angels, nor principalities, nor things present, nor things to come, nor powers, nor heights, nor depth, nor any other created thing, will be able to separate us from the love of God, which is in Christ Jesus our Lord. (Romans 8:38–39, emphasis mine)

As followers of Christ, we may know that God loves us. But have we really come to believe it? Are we convinced of it? Even the apostle John, who walked with the Lord while he was on earth, and the apostle Paul, who endured such persecution and suffering, needed to be convinced over and over again of the unfailing love of Christ before they really came to believe it and then walk in that understanding.

Regardless of where you are in your inward journey with the Lord, whether you are a new believer or a seasoned saint, this book has been written with the hope that our heavenly Bridegroom will use it to touch you, challenge you, and draw you by his love into a more intimate relationship with himself.

May the spiritual reality of the love portrayed between the Shulammite maiden and King Solomon be yours as you experientially come to know the love that the Lord Jesus, your heavenly king, has for you. "For truly, a greater than Solomon is here." (Luke 11:31, NKJV).

PART 1: INITIAL LOVE

"My Beloved is mine, and I am his."

SONG OF SONGS 2:16

"The whole world is not worth the day on which the Song of Songs was given to Israel, for all the Scriptures are holy, but the Song of Songs is the Holy of Holies."

RABBI AQIBA, FIRST HALF OF THE SECOND CENTURY

The Longing

SONG OF SONGS, CHAPTER 1

"May he kiss me with the kisses of his mouth!
For your love is better than wine.
Your oils have a pleasing fragrance,
Your name is like purified oil;
Therefore the maidens love you."

SONG OF SONGS 1:2–3

I was working in the fields on that day when I saw a chariot approaching from the distance, surrounded by ten soldiers on horseback. The day was hot, and the glare of the sun caused my eyes to squint as I looked in their direction. As the chariot passed by, the driver slowed the mare leading it and looked in my direction. Then he gently pulled on the reins and guided the lead mare until the chariot stopped very close to where I was standing. He stepped out and moved toward me.

I had never seen anyone like him before. He was young—about my own age—and had a distinct air of royalty about him. My first thought was that surely he would ask me for a drink or perhaps for directions. I could not conceive why else one such as he would come to this small, obscure village, much less pause in my field!

As he came closer, suddenly I could smell the sweet scent of the oil of anointing upon his head. It was vibrant and alive, a wafting fragrance that seemed to quicken the very air where I stood. He was dashing, with fine features and long, wavy hair the color of a raven.

The young man just stood there before me, staring at me with a penetrating gaze. I had the feeling somewhere in my innermost being that I had known him before. Yet I did not really know him at all. As I looked at his handsome face, I did not know how to interpret what was going on within him. His eyes seemed to swim with wonder, but I could not imagine why. It was almost as if he were smitten by love!

Suddenly he turned, went back to the chariot, mounted, and rode off. But even as he was leaving, I realized deep within myself that he had given me an unspoken message. Hope was rising in me. In that moment, I dared to believe that he would return.

As the last soldier in the convoy was passing by, I raised my arm and waved to him, calling out, "Who was that young man?"

Looking back over his shoulder as he rode off, the soldier shouted, "That was Solomon—the king!"

"Solomon," I breathed, in near disbelief.

Finishing my tasks in the field, I left early and returned to my home. All the while I considered the inexplicable event that had just taken place.

What was that look I had seen in his eyes? Could I trust my feelings? My mind seemed to contradict what I was feeling in my heart. *Certainly I have misinterpreted his gaze,* I said to myself. *It would be impossible for the king to have feelings of his own for one such as me.*

Still, I could not help but imagine. The wonder, the hope of seeing him again took root in my heart and grew stronger with each passing day. I realized that he had awakened something within me for which I longed, but only slowly did I come to understand. The king had awakened in me a desire for love!

I had grown up in the village and observed how the people in my community lived their lives, accepting as inevitable the traditions and the life inherited from their fathers and forefathers. They were poor folk, and life was difficult. They got up every morning and worked hard all day long in the fields, in the vineyards, or around their homes just to barely eke out a living. And then they got up the next morning to repeat the cycle all over again. Few ever strayed far from their roots of origin or had the opportunity to choose another path in life.

I also saw the frustrations and the deep dissatisfaction within them—and within myself—and did not wish to live this way. Surely, there must be something better. Surely, destiny must have a purpose higher than this for me. As I pondered this thought, I found myself, for the first time, daring to believe it.

What I did not know at the time was that the king shared my hopes and dreams. Although he had been born of royalty and had the whole kingdom at his fingertips, he too longed for an incomparable love—one unlike anything that he had known before.

In the following days, as I went about my daily chores in the field, my thoughts returned over and over to the king. In my daydreams, I could see him coming for me and the two of us running off together to be married, two lovers whose passions could no longer be contained.

Sometimes I would take a deep breath and imagine, once again, the intoxicating fragrance of the anointing oil. At other times, I would just allow the king's name to roll across my lips. *Solomon.* It was such a beautiful name—one that meant *peace.*

I had heard of the king from stories the villagers had told—of his wealth, his wisdom, and his winsome appearance. It was no wonder that this young monarch was the desire of every maiden in the kingdom!

But there was no one with whom I could talk about these intimate feelings. Finally, one day, simple but powerful words began to form within me. Like a flood, a prayer rose from somewhere deep in my being and poured out from my lips: "May he kiss me again and again with the kisses of his mouth!"

I closed my eyes and began to picture him standing before me once again. What would I say? What would I want to tell him? Then the words came: "Your love is sweeter than vintage wine! Your oils have a pleasing fragrance. The sound of your name is like the soft, gentle noise of a meadow brook. No wonder all the maidens love you!"

POINTS TO CONSIDER

Going deeper with the Lord begins with a longing. That longing is planted in a believer's heart by God himself.

The maiden in this song represents one who has already come to faith in Christ. The text tells us she is a maiden (a virgin). The word *maiden* or *virgin* speaks of those who have already placed their faith in Christ and been given eternal life, as we see in the words of the apostle Paul: "For I am jealous for you with a godly jealousy; for I betrothed you to one husband, so that to Christ I might present you as a pure virgin" (2 Corinthians 11:2).

The Song, therefore, begins with one who already loves the Lord—but who wants to be more intimate with him and does not want to settle for "life as normal" anymore. It begins with one who wants a rich, passionate life with the Lord and all that such a life entails.

Knowing Christ in such a way will bring changes and adventure. It is not the conservative path to take: there are many maidens, but few who long for a deeper life with him.

The maiden craved the king's kisses. She desired that he would show his affection and love by kissing her over and over again. For the believer, this corresponds to our yearning for the Lord to reveal his love for us over and over again and to demonstrate his affection. Each kiss we receive from him is a new revelation of who he is, communicating a fresh experience of his love.

The oils in verse 3 represent the heavenly scent of the virtues of Christ that we sense when we are in his presence. They speak of his character, his powerfully attractive nature, his righteousness, peace, faithfulness, strength, wisdom, and grace. Verse 3 can also be a reference to the healing oils put on wounds. In the story of the Good Samaritan, the Samaritan found a man in the ditch and bandaged him, pouring oil and wine on his wounds (Luke 10:33–34). Experiencing the presence of Christ not only brings intense enjoyment, but healing.

We cannot know God apart from revelation. Growing in the knowledge of him comes with having more and more revelation. Take, for example, Simon Peter and the story in Matthew 16:13–17:

> Now when Jesus came into the district of Caesarea Philippi, He was asking His disciples, "Who do people say that the Son of man is?" And they said, "Some say John the Baptist; and others, Elijah; but still others, Jeremiah, or one of the prophets." He said to them, "But who do you say that I am?" Simon Peter answered, "You are the Christ, the Son of the living God." And Jesus said to him, "Blessed are you, Simon Barjona, because flesh and blood did not reveal this to you, but My Father who is in heaven."

Peter knew the Lord and had walked with him, but it took the Father's revelation for him to see that this was the Messiah, the very Son of the living God.

So then, the Song of Songs begins with a prayer. It is a prayer asking for revelation: to know Christ in a more intimate way, and to know more of his love.

THOUGHTS/PRAYERS

Lord, kiss me. Kiss me over and over again. Show me your affection and love. I want to be more intimate with you. I need you to reveal yourself to me. Open my eyes that I may see you and know your affection for me. Soften my heart so that I will love you more. Put a longing in my heart to know you in ways deeper than I have ever known you before.

Your love is better than anything this world has to offer; tasting of your love, better than the sweetest wine. Being in your presence is far better than smelling the most fragrant anointing oils of a king. Your name is lovely, Lord Jesus. Satisfy the desire in my heart to know you more.

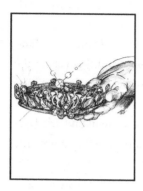

Drawn by Love

Song of Songs, Chapter 1

"Draw me after you and let us run together!
The king has brought me into his chambers."

Song of Songs 1:4a

I had gone, this day, to the orchard of nut trees to see the blossoms of the valley and to see whether the vine had budded. Suddenly I looked up, and there in the distance I saw the dust churning. My heart beat fast in hope! It was as if my prayer had called to him. It was the king!

His chariot pulled up beside my vineyard once more. The young king stepped forth. I could tell there was a certain eagerness in him, just as there was in me. I had no idea what he would say. Would his conversation be casual? Some observation, perhaps, about the day or the weather?

Then he spoke. His very first words were direct and clear: "Would you come with me into the city? I would like to show you the place where I live."

For a moment, I was speechless. I had not expected such an odd beginning. What was this? Was he inviting me into his very home?

"My king, surely you do not mean now—at this moment?" I stammered.

He was smiling, his whole face alive with excitement. "Yes, I do!" he replied.

"But…but… I must return to my home and change my clothes. My hands are dirty, and I must wash and—"

"Give it no thought," he said. "Nor should you be afraid. Be assured that you will not come to any place that will be inappropriate. My charioteers will have you home by nightfall."

Strangely, although reason argued that this was an absurd thing to do, I felt as if I were enveloped in a cloud of peace. I trusted the young man.

"But, sir," I protested faintly, "I have never before even ridden in a chariot. I—"

Instantly, he jumped up into his chariot. "Give me your hand," he said, extending his.

Smiling with the daring of it all, I took the leap. I grasped his hand tightly, and immediately he hoisted me up. He laughed aloud, as did I, at the outrageousness, the thrill, the absurdity of what had just taken place. I could not help but think, *Where will this adventure lead?*

The chariot began to move. I grasped its rails. He seized the reins and cried out to the horses, and in a moment they broke into a gallop. I think even they sensed the excitement!

The wind blew against my face as the horses raced before us. I was standing in a chariot trimmed with gold beside the king! I laughed again with exhilaration. Above the noise of the horses' hooves, the vibrations of the chariot from the ruts in the road, and the wheels grinding upon the small rocks, the king leaned in my direction and shouted, "On to Jerusalem!" I could barely contain the joy I felt. Though in truth I had only just met him, I felt so secure and protected.

As we approached the gleaming walls of the palace, I began to hear loud calls and commands. They seemed to come from everywhere. Trumpets blasted on every side, announcing the king's arrival. Guards, arrayed in military attire with swords strapped to their sides, bowed before him and then stepped back and opened the large bronze gates leading to the palace. I felt suddenly very sun-browned, and I hid my hands, stained with the juice and dirt of the vineyards, in my skirts. *They all must think that the king has just purchased a slave—someone of the lowliest rank.* Yet that was not at all how he treated me.

As we entered the courtyard, the horses slowed and came to a halt. He offered his hand once more, and the two of us dismounted. My eyes looked up at the palace. The immense white stone blocks reflecting the sunlight, the columns, the magnificent architecture—it all took my breath away!

We did not go immediately inside. Instead, the king led me through the courtyard and down a path until we came to an iron gate. Opening the gate, we went inside. It was a garden. Not just a garden, but the most exquisite garden one could imagine. Date and almond trees, ornamental bushes, henna flowers, and the heady scent of jasmine—I could hardly take it all in, and the details escaped me almost as fast as they came to me. He spoke hardly a word. He simply wanted me to behold the lush setting. It was unspeakably beautiful. But upon reflection, I could scarce remember what I had seen.

I have often been asked what I saw that day—what I heard, what I was shown, where I was taken. To these questions I have only been able to answer, "The king stood beside me that day. How could I possibly know?"

Our next destination was a balcony inside the palace, which overlooked the site upon which the holy temple was being constructed. From there, Solomon pointed out the growing structures and explained to me that this would be a temple like none other, the place where another king would one day dwell—the King of all kings.

Then, leaning on the rail, he asked, "Do you like the view from here?"

"It is magnificent! There is no view like it in all of Jerusalem," I replied.

He smiled, obviously pleased with my answer. "Few have stood where you stand to look upon this. But I have plans to improve upon it," he said. "For when the temple is complete, this palace will be dwarfed in comparison to the one I intend to build."

There was more that he wanted to show me, so we turned and went back inside. My heart was full of wonder—but even more full of joy, just to be near him, to be hearing his plans as though I were a trusted friend. Walking alongside me, he said, "I now wish to take you into the place where none of the gardeners and only a few of my servants have ever been. Only I and my most trusted guards and servants can walk here. I shall take you inside the castle walls, show you the high towers and the bulwarks, and then show you the place that is mine alone."

I marveled as he took me up and down the stone stairs and through the corridors. Guards were everywhere. It seemed as if gold was everywhere as well—golden statues, candlesticks, and tables. Finally, he stopped in front of a large wooden door. Beside the door, a tall soldier stood guard silently. His large arms were folded across his chest. He was mammoth in build, with shoulders and biceps rippling with muscle.

"Here is the inmost portion of the palace," the king said with an eager smile. "It is my home; it is my secret place. I would have you see it!"

Pushing the door open, he took me by the hand and we stepped inside. I looked around. It was the king's bedroom! In the center of the room and against the stone wall was a large, magnificent bed. Never could I have imagined anything like it. It was upheld on its four corners by posts of ivory, from which hung the most beautiful tapestry of curtains my eyes had ever beheld. Their beauty was resplendent. The hues of blue, violet, and mauve were the work of a master artist.

On one side of the bed were steps leading up to a pool that was the king's bath. On the other side of the bed was a dark piece of wooden furniture, upon which sat the king's golden crown.

"Is that the crown you wear when you sit on your throne?" I asked.

"Yes," he said with a smile. Then he walked over, picked it up, and brought it back to show me. It was exquisite, bedecked with multicolored jewels.

"Go ahead. Touch it," he said as he smiled proudly and extended the crown toward me.

I reached out cautiously, touching the crown and letting my fingers glide slowly over the ridges. I marveled at the green, blue, and red jewels which were inlaid so beautifully within its smooth, shiny surface.

He returned the crown to its place and rejoined me.

We only stayed in the bedroom for a moment. Then, without a word, he motioned toward the door and led me back through the palace and out into the courtyard where we had first arrived. He signaled to the guards. Within moments a chariot pulled up to his side, driven by two handsome, magnificently robed charioteers. The king gently grasped my head between his hands, leaned over, and placed a soft parting kiss on my forehead.

"Return the maiden to her home," he commanded.

Before they could respond, the king turned suddenly. Someone was approaching. The stranger waved one hand in the air, motioning the charioteers to stop. He was a short, round man with a balding head. He held pen in one hand and parchment in the other. *He must be the one charged with recording the king's daily activities,* I thought.

"My king, where have you been, and what have you been doing this day?" the scribe asked with a smile.

The king stepped over to me, lifted my hand gently from the rail, and kissed the back of my hand.

"Where I have been? What I have done? What I have seen? This most beautiful of maidens has stood beside me this day. How could I possibly know?"

POINTS TO CONSIDER

When we first come to Christ, we know him as our Savior, the one who saves us from sin and gives eternal life. But we often fail to realize that he is also the king. He is the King of all kings and wants not only to be our Savior, but our lord and our lover.

The maiden no sooner asked for the king's kisses—his displays of affection—than her prayers were answered. The text says, "The *king* brought me into his chambers." For the believer who wants to be more intimate with the Lord, one of the first revelations to receive is that he is the king! He is not just a casual friend. He is not one to go to, ask for advice, and then take it or leave it. He is the king! And he wants to be lord over every area of a believer's life.

From the maiden's testimony, we can see that she had tasted of the wine that this world has to offer, but had left it behind. Once she had tasted of the king's love, she quickly discovered there was no comparison!

Any maiden who got near to the presence of Solomon loved to breathe in the smell of his pleasing, costly fragrances. Any believer who has ever spent time in the presence of Christ and has been "kissed" with the displays of his affection wants to be drawn closer to him.

The Song of Songs, from beginning to end, reveals how the Lord continually draws a believer to himself. This drawing is one of its major themes:

- "Draw me… " (Song of Songs 1:4)
- "The king has brought me into his chambers." (Song of Songs 1:4)
- "Go forth on the trail of the flock." (Song of Songs 1:8)
- "He has brought me into his banqueting hall." (Song of Songs 2:4)
- "Arise, come along." (Song of Songs 1:10)
- "Arise, come along." (Song of Songs 2:13)
- "A voice, knocking, open to me…" (Song of Songs 5:2)
- "Come let us go…" (Song of Songs 7:11)

In the New Testament, Jesus told his disciples:

"No one can come to me unless the father who sent me draws him; and I will raise him up on the last day." (John 6:44)

"And I, if I am lifted up from the earth, will draw all men to myself." (John 12:32)

"You did not choose me but I chose you, and appointed you that you would go and bear fruit, and that your fruit would remain." (John 15:16)

Verse 4 says, "Draw me after you and let us run together." The obvious meaning here would be that the maiden wants the king to draw her so that the two of them may run off together (elope). However, the preceding verse mentions other maidens. A secondary interpretation could be, "If you draw me, not only will I run after you, but these other maidens will run after you together with me." In the Christian life, this principle is clearly applied: when the Lord draws someone to himself, others will follow.

One example of this principle is in the lives of Mary and Martha. John 11 tells the story of Jesus raising Lazarus from the dead. When Martha heard that Jesus was coming, she went to meet him to see why he hadn't come earlier. Leaving Jesus, the chapter tells us, "She went away and called Mary her sister, saying secretly, 'The Teacher is here and is calling for you'" (John 11:28). The Jews who were with Mary in the house were consoling her, but "when they saw that Mary got up quickly and went out, they followed her" (John 11:31). No one followed Martha when she went out on her own to meet Jesus, but Mary was drawn by the Lord, and when she responded, others in the house followed.

THOUGHTS/PRAYERS

Lord Jesus, you are not only my Savior, but my King. I want you to rule over every area of my life, and for those areas I am not willing to give up, make me willing, for you are a God of love. Draw me to that inner, sacred place deep within me, to my spirit where the human meets the divine; and let me hear you; let me see you. You are the King, and I want you to occupy your rightful place in my life as King and Lord. Draw me, Lord, and I will run after you.

Day Three

Self-Discovery

Song of Songs, Chapter 1

"I am black but lovely,
O daughters of Jerusalem,
Like the tents of Kedar,
Like the curtains of Solomon."

Song of Songs 1:5

I returned home late that afternoon, before dark as the king had promised. The villagers came out of their homes and stopped their daily tasks to see the royal chariot roll through the village and stop in front of my home. Word had spread that I had been whisked away by the king that morning.

During the whole ride home, I continued to muse over this extraordinary, unexpected encounter with the king. I wondered how I would explain it to my family, my friends. I tried to clear my head and put in perspective all that had just happened. But the truth was, everything that had happened was so wondrous that my head would not clear at all!

The charioteers pulled up in front of my small house. One of them stepped out, turned, and lifted his hand to me. I took it and stepped down, and he escorted me to the door. I ducked inside the one dark room of my family's house. No one was home. I sat down on a rickety wooden chair and stared at the dirt floor. My emotions were confused. I wanted to wail. I wanted to cry. I wanted to laugh out loud. I felt afraid; afraid that my poor heart was falling in love with the king. Yet, where I lived, kings did not fall in love with such as I.

I lifted my eyes and saw the tiny, tattered cloth hanging over the room's solitary window. *What a staggering contrast,* I thought, calling up images of the king's chambers and the magnificence of the palace.

Suddenly, there was a rap at the door. I rose up, went to the door, and opened it. There stood a company of the other young women from the village, nervously laughing and begging to be invited inside.

"Is it true?" one asked when they were hardly through the door. "Were you really taken to Jerusalem, to the palace of the king?"

"Yes, it is true," I responded.

"Tell us everything! Tell us what you saw, where you went, what it was like to be with him!"

I could not help but smile at their giddiness. After all, these were my friends! "Everyone sit down," I said. "I will tell you what it was like to be with the king!"

My joy flooded back to me as I recounted every detail I could remember. "Rejoice with me and be glad," I said in my exuberance. "The king is everything you could ever imagine and more!"

Then one of them leaned forward and asked, "But why you? What does he see in you? All the other maidens of the kingdom are at his disposal. He could choose any one of them to be his bride."

I sensed a trace of jealousy in her voice. And the words hit me hard—*bride. His bride.* Was that truly what he wanted?

Then another chimed in, "Queens are beautiful and royally dressed. They have soft, tender skin because they bathe in milk and oils and precious perfumes. But you work continually out in the hot sun. Your hands are calloused. Your skin is weathered and burned. How could the king overlook this?"

By now, scorn, sarcasm, and disdain were all whirling around the room. I could see it coming from their eyes.

I was humiliated, and my confusion had returned—and grown even stronger. Their piercing statements expressed the very thoughts that had been churning around in my own mind from the first day he saw me in the field. Spoken aloud, they made an awful truth. My heart began to break.

My hair fell over my face as I bowed my head and wept. "It is true. It is true," I said, as my chest convulsed and I tried to hold back the tears. "I am black, like the dirty, dusty goat hairs that cover the shepherd's tents of Kedar. I know I am not worthy to even come near to the king." I remembered my hands as the chariot pulled up to the palace; my thoughts—*They must think he has purchased a slave girl.* But he had been so courteous. I drew myself up as best as I could, wiped my cheeks, and said, "Why this happened to me, I will never know. He has probably already forgotten me, and I will never see his face again. But it has been a wonderful day nonetheless."

No sooner had I spoken these words than the reverie of my experience began to creep back into my thoughts. I saw him, his youthful, enthusiastic hand extended to me; his eyes sparkling and kind. My mind's eye returned to the spot where I had last seen him, where he had tenderly and lovingly kissed me on my forehead. I remembered the look on his face and the feeling in my heart. Instinctively, I knew that he must have felt the same way too. But it was incredible! Why was he blinded to my faults and shortcomings; why did he not seem to care where I had come from? For some inexplicable reason, he saw in me beauty, not blackness.

Grasping this new reality, I slowly looked up once again to the company of maidens. A smile cut across the stream of tears on my face. I felt color returning to my cheeks and knew there was a sparkle in my moistened eyes. I cleared my throat and spoke in a slow but steady voice, addressing my gawking onlookers.

"But I see something else now. Your words are true. Yes, I am black. Yes, my hands are rough. Yes, my face has been baked by the sun. But I ask you this question: which one of us is to say that such things are not lovely in the eyes of the king? Who will ultimately decide what is beautiful, what is shameful? Are you, here in this room, my judges? Beauty is not my standard or yours to decide."

Sensing the truth of my own words, I became even bolder. "I will tell you exactly who decides what beauty is. It is the king himself. Yes, I am black, but I am also lovely. I am swarthy, but I am also as striking to the king as the exquisite curtains that adorn his very own bedchamber!"

POINTS TO CONSIDER

The Lord "kissed her" again, and she received another revelation: "I am black but lovely." When the Lord shows us who he is—fabulously rich, high, and exalted—in the light of his greatness, we, like the maiden, will also realize who we are.

The prophet Isaiah saw the Lord and immediately realized that he was a man of unclean lips and an unclean race (Isaiah 6:5). Yet, he also realized that God was choosing him for a special work. So too, after seeing the king, the maiden knew that she was black, but also lovely. The two revelations go hand in hand.

The apostle Paul also gives us a clear understanding of these competing truths:

- In Ephesians 1:1, he began his letter saying, "Paul, an apostle of Jesus Christ," but in chapter 3, verse 8, he is "the least of all the saints."
- In 1 Corinthians 15:9, Paul recognizes his own apostleship—a high spiritual calling—though he sees himself as "the least of the apostles." But in 2 Corinthians 12:11 he is a "nobody."
- In 1 Timothy 1:12–15, he thanked the Lord for considering him faithful and

putting him into service, while in the same breath acknowledging that "It is a trustworthy statement, deserving full acceptance, that Christ Jesus came into the world to save sinners, among whom I am foremost."

- In Romans 6 and elsewhere, Paul said that we are "in Christ" and "united with him," but in the following chapter he wrestled with the realization that sin dwelt in his flesh and that evil was present in him.

The temptation for the maiden was to try to make herself more beautiful for Solomon so that she would be acceptable to him, as we will subsequently see. But she was altogether beautiful to him just the way she was. His love would draw her and purify her, making her into what she could only hope, at this time, to be.

THOUGHTS/PRAYERS

Precious Lord, I humbly acknowledge that you are robed in light and that you are holy and without peer. You are one of a kind: the best and beyond compare. There is no one like you. In your light I am nothing. Knowing that gives me a sense of nakedness and realization that I am unworthy to be the object of your affections. But you paid a great price to purchase me and redeem me with your precious blood. In your eyes, I am now forgiven, holy, and blameless. Keep me humbly aware of who I am without you. At the same time, continue to show me who I am *in* you, and let me live in your borrowed light.

Day Four

Delivered from
Distracting Service

SONG OF SONGS, CHAPTER 1

"Do not stare at me because I am swarthy,
For the sun has burned me.
My mother's sons were angry with me;
They made me caretaker of the vineyards,
But I have not taken care of my own vineyard."

SONG OF SONGS 1:6

As I waited for the king's return, the days slipped into weeks. Why had he not come back? I struggled with longing, hope, and fear. I grew more aware of my weather-beaten, work-hardened skin. But I told myself, "I am lovely. To him, I am lovely."

Through hard work, my family had accumulated several small vineyards on the hills around our village. I returned to work in my own plot, the sacred ground where I had first met the king. I often found myself alone, absorbed in thought and stopping to sit for minutes—or hours—at a time, neglecting my work as my thoughts drifted back to the enchanting day I had spent with the monarch who had stolen my heart.

Seeing my lethargy, my brothers became increasingly intolerant of my behavior. "Come," one of them snapped, "there is much work to do. We need your help in the other vineyards. If you work with us, your joy will return, and you will forget all of this foolishness of dreaming that one day he will return. My sister, you cannot truly believe that you will become a queen. Forget this folly."

Gradually, their coaxes turned into threats. In the end, their anger was no longer masked. They forced me to come with them to labor in the vineyards where they toiled.

The work was demanding. It was the season for pruning the vines and tying the remaining branches to the trellises. I worked from morning until night. But soon I became accustomed to the long hours and the responsibilities they put upon me. Gradually, they increased my tasks. I was also put in charge of caring for the young goats. Although consumed with work, finally, after seeing some fruit start to appear on the vines, I began to derive some meager pleasure from all my toil. Gradually, my deep longings for the king were covered over with some sense of purpose and worth from the work of my hands.

As I returned home late one afternoon with my small flock of young kid goats, I decided to pass by my own vineyard. I had not visited it in quite some time. When I arrived, I was startled to find it in such disarray. The ground was thirsty and dry. It was overgrown with weeds. The poles upon which the vines had woven themselves were drooping and had not been shored up. Nor had the vines been pruned. Their beautiful but unfruitful branches grew wildly everywhere. The protective hedge surrounding my vineyard had been trampled in numerous places. The deer, foxes, and other creatures had found their way in, looking for food.

Exhausted and hungry from another long, hot, grueling day, I stared at the unkempt vineyard. Tears sprang to my eyes. This had been such a place of dreaming—but was now such a place of ruin. The sun beat on my head, and my heart wrenched at the thought of returning to my brothers and their harsh ways.

Thinking that I was alone, I spoke aloud, "O my pitiful vineyard, how painful it is to look at you now! You remind me of the condition of my own heart and how I have neglected the hopes and dreams of ever finding the one whom my soul loves again. If I could but see him once more, I would ask of him where he pastures his flock and gives it rest in the heat of the day."

"Ask me, and I will tell you," interrupted a familiar voice from behind me.

I whirled around. There he was! He was dressed in a simple but elegant sleeveless white tunic and sandals.

"You are here!" I exclaimed. "You were listening to me?"

"I have passed by this place many times since I last saw you, hoping to find you. But when you did not appear and I saw that your vineyard had been overtaken with weeds and thorn bushes, I thought that you must have gone away. I was beginning to believe you were gone forever. But I decided to return one more time today."

"I am so embarrassed that you have found me in such a state," I said in return. "Please, do not stare at me. When the others from my village look at me, I want to hide from them as well. I sometimes even want to veil myself and cover my face as one who mourns so that you, and anyone else who sees me, will not perceive the emptiness I feel inside."

"I can tell that you have been working hard," he said kindly. "I know that you have missed me. You are tired. You are hungry. And you are thirsty. That is nothing to be ashamed of. But you have not been to this place in a long time. If you had come back sooner, I would have found you and taken you away again, for I could not stop thinking about you. To me, you are still the most beautiful among all women!"

POINTS TO CONSIDER

For the Christian, "my mother's sons" represent other believers in the family of God, who are our brothers and sisters in Christ.

Often, it is the ones who really love the Lord and are running after him who are most susceptible to being taken advantage of by some who hold positions of authority in churches or Christian organizations. Leaders can recognize those who are zealous and really want to serve the Lord, and they will recruit them, putting them to work in what appears to be genuine Christian service. But after time, this can lead to loss of joy, disillusionment, exhaustion, spiritual hunger, and sometimes burnout. All of the time-consuming activity can become a distraction, causing the lover of God to neglect care of his or her own spiritual life.

When this happens, it is time to return to first love.

We see this in the message to the Ephesian church in the Book of Revelation:

To the angel of the church in Ephesus write: The One who holds the seven stars in His right hand, the One who walks among the seven golden lampstands, says this: "I know your deeds and your toil and perseverance, and that you cannot tolerate evil men, and you put to the test those who call themselves apostles, and they are not and you found them to be false; and you have perseverance and have endured for My name's sake, and have not grown weary. But I have this against you, that you have left your first love. Therefore remember from where you have fallen, and repent and do the deeds that you did at first; or else I am coming to you and will remove your lampstand out of its place—unless you repent. Yet this you do have, that you hate the deeds of the Nicolaitans, which I also hate. (Revelation 2:1–7)

There were many things that the Ephesian church was doing well:

- They were involved in serving the Lord.
- They had perseverance.

- They had the backbone not to tolerate evil men in their midst.
- They stood up to those who pretended to be apostles and leaders, but who were not.
- They endured under persecution.
- They hated things that the Lord hates.

Still, they were on the brink of having their testimony removed completely. The reason given is that this was a matter of love. They were going through the motions and doing what outwardly appeared to be all the right things, but they had left their first love.

Service should come as a response to spending time with the Lord and then responding to what he is doing within you.

What counts is *not* how much we can do for God, but how much *God* can do working in and through us.

Many institutions today were birthed by the Lord in the beginning, but are now the dead coral reefs of the Christian religion—a creeping growth of something that was once alive, but is now dead.

There is hope for those who feel pressured to maintain an inordinate amount of spiritual responsibility, though inwardly they know they are running on empty. Others have walked that lonely road. The maiden was one of them.

THOUGHTS/PRAYERS

Lord Jesus, if there is anything or anyone that is distracting me from knowing you; if there is any service that I am performing that I think will impress you, but that has caused my heart to grow cold; then I ask you to put your finger on it. Reveal it to me and bring me back to my first love. Replace any idols of empty ministry activity and Christian service with a passionate pursuit of you alone.

Finding the True Flock
and Shepherds of Grace

Song of Songs, Chapter 1
"Tell me, O you whom my soul loves,
Where do you pasture your flock,
Where do you make it lie down at noon?
For why should I be like one who veils herself
Beside the flocks of your companions?"

"If you yourself do not know,
Most beautiful among women,
Go forth on the trail of the flock
And pasture your young goats
By the tents of the shepherds."

Song of Songs 1:7–8

The most beautiful of women! I thought. Could his words really have been sincere?

Consoled and reassured that my thoughts of his love for me were not a lie, I opened my heart to the king and sought his counsel. "Your eyes see through me. You know how much I am in need of rest and nourishment for my soul, as are these young kids. Tell me, what am I to do? Do you know where I—where they—can find pasture and shade to lie down in the scorching heat of the day?"

"You are like a sheep that has been mistreated by its shepherds," he replied in a soft, caring voice. "There are those who are harsh and demanding, shepherds in name only. There are those who cling violently to laws and rules and seek to impose them on others, yet they too are called shepherds. But I have my own trustworthy shepherds who pasture my flocks not far from here. They are not like your brothers, who lack compassion and grace and who burden and overwork the one for whom they should be caring. My shepherds have been trained well. They are good shepherds. Some of them are quite young, some are old, but they are full of wisdom and grace for those who seek their help."

"Where did these good shepherds come from? How is it that you can trust them all?" I asked.

"Do you recall the greatest of all shepherds, my father, David? He was a man with a tender love in his bosom for every lamb. He was willing to risk his own life to fight lions and bears with his bare hands in order to protect them. These shepherds of whom I speak were taught by my father and other shepherds whose lives he sculpted. But my father received his instruction from an even greater shepherd—the one he called, 'Lord.' God was the one who provided for his needs, gave him rest in green pastures and drink beside quiet waters, restored his soul, led him in paths of righteousness, set a banquet before him in the presence of his enemies, and walked with him through the valley where death dwells. If men can be taught to care for such simple and dumb creatures, how much more, if they have the shepherd heart of David and David's Lord, will they care for those who were created in God's very image?"

"Will you take me to them?" I asked him.

"The shadows are growing long, and I must return to the city," the king replied. "But in the morning, at daybreak, arise, gather your flock, and point them in the direction of Jerusalem. Soon you will come to the trail of my flocks. Follow that trail until you come to the tents of the shepherds.

"On my way back to the palace, I will tell them to prepare for your arrival. They will welcome you and care for you. They will feed you with raisin cakes, and your strength will return. They will give you rest and show you where to pasture your young goats. I will return to meet you there. I will not be gone long."

POINTS TO CONSIDER

Serving the Lord in our own strength can only result in spiritual exhaustion and emptiness. When the realization dawns that we have been doing this, it is time to return to a place of rest and find a renewed enjoyment and strength in Christ himself. It is time to make a choice to cease working for the Lord and move in the direction of allowing the Lord to work in and through you.

In spite of the fact that the maiden was tired, hungry, and groping to find rest for her soul, she was still the most beautiful among women to the king. Every time he addressed her throughout the Song—no matter what stage of spiritual growth she was in—he always saw her as his beautiful one, his perfect one.

- "Most beautiful among women." (Song of Songs 1:8)
- "How beautiful you are, my darling." (Song of Songs 1:15)
- "Arise, my darling, my beautiful one, and come along." (Song of Songs 2:10)
- "Arise, my darling, my beautiful one, and come along!" (Song of Songs 2:13)
- "How beautiful you are, my darling, how beautiful you are." (Song of Songs 4:1)
- "You are altogether beautiful, my darling, and there is no blemish in you." (Song of Songs 4:7)
- "How beautiful is your love, my sister, my bride!" (Song of Songs 4:10)
- "Open to me, my sister, my darling, my dove, my perfect one!" (Song of Songs 5:2)
- "You are as beautiful as Tirzah, my darling, as lovely as Jerusalem, as awesome as an army with banners." (Song of Songs 6:4)
- "But my dove, my perfect one, is unique." (Song of Songs 6:9)
- "How beautiful are your feet in sandals, O prince's daughter!" (Song of Songs 7:1)
- "How beautiful and how delightful you are, my love, with all your charms!" (Song of Songs 7:6)
- "Come, my beloved, let us go into the country." (Song of Songs 7:11)
- "I want you to swear, O daughters of Jerusalem, do not arouse or awaken my love until she pleases." (Song of Songs 8:4)

When God sees us, he sees us as having been washed by the blood of Christ, which has made us perfectly righteous and holy in his sight. He sees us "in Christ" (1 Corinthians 1:30). He looks at us and loves us in exactly the same way as he does his precious Son. We are part of the divine family.

When the king speaks to his maiden, there is no trace of disappointment or condemnation. He was not angry with her as were her "mother's sons." He was not overly concerned with her inadequacies. He did not put her down or compare her to others. She was unique—and loved.

The Lord is passionately in love with us just the way we are. He formed each one of us in our mother's womb. We were fearfully and wonderfully made. We were endowed with unique personalities, gifts, and talents, all designed to uniquely magnify him.

In Psalm 3:3, the psalmist said, "You are my glory and the One who lifts my head!" The Lord Jesus does not want us wallowing in the dust, nor looking down in shame. He wants to put his finger under our chin, lift it up, and cause us to look into his face, where we will hear the words, "You are beautiful, my darling, and there is no blemish in you."

The tired, hungry Christian who has been under the influence of harsh shepherds and serving the Lord in an environment of rules, obligations, and laws needs to see that the Lord has his own shepherds of grace. And he has his own flock consisting of those who follow the Lamb wherever he goes (Revelation 14:4).

These shepherds may be living or they may be deceased. You may never meet them in this life. But they have left their tracks for you to follow. Consider some of the spiritual giants who, through the ages, have left their writings for future generations to feed upon: people like John Bunyan, Madame Guyon, Fenelon, Brother Lawrence, Watchman Nee, and scores of others. True shepherds of grace are those who can lead others into the experience of following the Spirit, resting in Christ, and feeding on him.

THOUGHTS/PRAYERS

Mary of Bethany was one who fed on Christ as she sat at his feet (Luke 10:39). Peter learned the lesson that before serving the Lord, he needed to first allow the Lord to serve him by washing his feet (John 13:5–6). Before we can adequately serve others, we need the Lord to refresh and fill us so that, out of fullness, we will have something to give.

Lord, guide my soul through the leading of your Spirit to those who are shepherds of grace, that I may learn where to find rest and nourishment in you. Lead me to a flock of believers whom you are shepherding so that, with them, I can follow you wherever you go.

Thank you that you are not only the good shepherd, but you are the pasture and the door by which I enter. You are the one I feed upon. Refresh me. Wash the dirt that I have accumulated from walking through this world off my feet, and fill me. Thank you that, even in those times when I struggle to find you, I am still, and always, your beautiful one.

The Promise of Transformation

SONG OF SONGS, CHAPTER 1

"To me, my darling, you are like
My mare among the chariots of Pharaoh.
Your cheeks are lovely with ornaments,
Your neck with strings of beads.
We will make for you ornaments of gold
With beads of silver."

"While the king was at his table,
My perfume gave forth its fragrance."

SONG OF SONGS 1:9–12

That night I prepared a small cloth bag with some of my belongings—a change of clothes, a comb, a brush, and some bread and dried figs to eat along the way. My mother was concerned for me, but I told her not to worry. I assured her that I would be safe.

The next morning, I arose before sunrise. My mother heard me stirring and got up to see if there was anything I needed. I moved toward the door and opened it a crack so that I could see her face in the dark room, for the sun's rays were just beginning to lighten the skies.

"There is something I wish to give you to take with you on your journey," she said with a quivering smile. I had told her that the king had promised to meet me when I joined his shepherds, and though she could hardly believe it, her eyes were full of hope for me. Opening her hands, she produced two small strings of beads, a tiny vial containing a vestige of perfume that had not been opened in years, and a pair of pendant earrings. They were her only treasures. "Take these," she said.

"They are not much, but they are all I have. I want you to have them for this special occasion."

I thanked her and placed them in my bag. Giving her a long embrace and a kiss, I slipped out the door and headed to the pen where our small flock of goats still slept.

I picked up my staff which lay against the rails of the wooden pen and hung the cloth bag by its strap over my shoulder. I felt invigorated as I opened the gate, let the goats out, and walked behind them into the sunrise down the dusty road which led to Jerusalem.

By midmorning, I came across a wide swath of tracks that cut across the road. My heart leapt. I knew I must be close to finding the shepherds. Veering off the road to the left, I quickened my pace and chased the small flock ahead of me, gently nudging some of the stragglers with my staff. About a half hour later, I came to a large, open field between two gently rolling hills that were sparsely strewn with rocks and wild olive trees. There in the field was a sea of sheep and goats. I gazed at the numbers of them in amazement. This, no doubt, was the king's own flock.

As I drew closer, I counted perhaps a dozen tents belonging to the shepherds. One by one, from different places in the field, they saw me coming and came to greet me.

The shepherds showed me where to leave my flock and then accompanied me to the tent in which I was to stay. They had placed a jar of water, a bowl, and a towel on a small table inside the tent next to the straw mat where I was to sleep. After freshening up a bit, I joined them for a lunch they had prepared: raisin cakes, apples, dried figs, lamb and fowl, and warm bread.

I sat talking with them all afternoon. They were delightful company: gentle men with many stories to tell. I learned much about their manner of tending the sheep and goats, how they nurtured them and cared for their wounds. But I also questioned them about the king, and they were quick to share with me more about his character and his ways. I inquired of them when the king would be arriving. They informed me that he would be coming to see me the following day.

We had dinner that night around a campfire. The night was cool; the night sky dark and clear, spangled with stars. When it was time to retire, I lit the wick of a small oil lamp from a partially burned stick. I excused myself, and with the lamp held out in the palm of my hand, I followed its light back to my tent. Once inside, I was in no hurry to sleep. For what seemed like a long while, I slowly paced around my temporary abode, anticipating the king's arrival and indulging in the tent's spaciousness and the luxury of having it all to myself, unlike the crowded one-room home in which I lived with my mother and brothers.

Waking with the dawn, my heart began to fill with excitement with the first blink of my eyelids. Today I would see the king once again! I rose, hastily dressed, and went out for a light breakfast with the shepherds. I then returned to my tent, washed, and pulled from my bag the only nice dress that I possessed. I slipped it on. I placed a dash of my mother's perfume along each side of my neck and behind my ears. Then I devoted an extraordinary amount of time to combing my hair, making sure every strand was in its proper place. Next, I lifted the two small strings of beads over my head and let them fall around my neck. Lastly, I fastened the two pendant earrings in my ears.

At that moment, I heard a loud shout from one of the shepherds. "The king is coming!"

I composed myself and emerged from my tent to meet him. I could see him coming in the distance. He was riding on a gorgeous white horse—a meticulously groomed, majestic creature. The horse had a leather bridle studded with an array of colorful jewels and a multicolored cloth with bobbing tassels of precious stones hanging from its neck. Flanking the king were two equally royal-looking men whom I did not recognize.

When they arrived, the king quickly dismounted from his horse in a puff of dust and walked directly toward me. "Greetings, fair maiden!" he said with a broad smile. "Have the shepherds treated you well?"

"Yes, they have, my king," I replied, smiling back at him. "I have learned so much from them already—not only about goats and sheep, but also about you!"

He chuckled.

"Do you feel rested? Has your strength returned?" he asked.

"Yes, my king," I said. "I am feeling about as strong as that regal steed you have been riding!"

"Then you must be endowed with great natural strength," he said as he turned to pat his horse on the neck. Looking back at me, he continued, "This is my prize mare, chief of all the forty thousand that belong to me. This beautiful animal used to serve at the front of a company of horses that pulled Pharaoh's royal chariot. Normally, the best of the horses from Egypt bring a high price, as much as one hundred shekels of silver. But for this exquisite animal, I paid one hundred and fifty shekels. Not only is she prized for her natural beauty, but she has been broken and trained, and she is submissive to my every wish. We were made for each other. I respect her and treat her well, as she does me."

Moving closer to me he said, "To me, my darling, you are like my mare among the chariots of Pharaoh."

I blushed. The king kept looking at me, and embarrassment wrestled with excitement deep within me.

My hair was pulled high over my head, revealing my prominent cheekbones. Gazing at them, he commented tenderly, "Your cheeks are lovely, and your earrings set them aflame with fire."

Then, looking at the strings of beads with which I had decorated my neck, he said, "Your neck, too, is lovely with strings of beads. But we will make for you ornaments of gold with beads of silver!"

His eyes went back to my own, and I realized that, although he had graciously complimented my adornments, they were not what drew him to me. He was looking at *me*—not at the things I had donned to please him.

The shepherds had been busily preparing a meal for the king, the two other guests, and me. Looking out from the tent where we were to eat, one of them motioned to the king that the feast was ready. The king extended his arm to me. I took it, and he escorted me inside the tent.

We reclined on separate couches which faced one another. Between us, yet within reach, were several low tables laden with food and drink.

To my surprise, I felt very much at ease with the king and these two distinguished gentlemen. Our conversation was as a feast: plentiful, filling, stimulating, and spiced with laughter. Although I came from a much lower station in life, they made me feel as if I were at home among them.

As we were finishing our meal, a gentle gust blew through the tent in the direction of King Solomon. The light wind seemed to snatch the fragrance from the perfume on my neck and carry it to him. Looking up, the king closed his eyes and breathed in the delicate scent. Then he turned to me with a lingering look and said, "The fragrance from your perfume is delightful. None of the pleasing aromas coming from this meal we have just eaten can compare. The smell of your perfume is by far the best, and the one which I most enjoy!"

POINTS TO CONSIDER

Comparing the maiden to his mare among the chariots of Pharaoh was a poetic way of saying that although she was running after the king, the maiden was still serving in her own natural strength. For a mare to be useful it needs to be broken and disciplined, with all its energies harnessed and directed.

The maiden realized that she was black, but lovely, and that she had been burned by the sun. In her eyes, her beauty needed to be improved upon so that she would be acceptable to the king, so she clad herself with her own handmade ornaments and beads.

Often, our tendency is to think that there must be something we can do outwardly that will make us more acceptable, more pleasing to the Lord than we already are, when, in fact, there is nothing we can do to make the Lord love us one drop more than he already does.

Attending more meetings, having longer quiet times each morning, engaging in more Bible study, prayers and fasting each week, increased tithing, community service, and missions trips, working harder at keeping the Ten Commandments—none of these things can earn a person more of the Lord's love.

The king noticed the maiden's string of beads, but he also promised her that they would be replaced by something else that "we will make"—"ornaments of gold with beads of silver." The "we" here is the triune God. The gold represents the divine nature. The silver represents redemption.

The promise for the Christian is that we will be adorned with a beauty that does not come from self-effort. Our beauty will be a result of the divine nature of God and the redemptive nature of Christ being worked into us through the transforming work of the Holy Spirit.

In New Testament terms, the maiden began to see the New Covenant promises. She began to grasp something of the "I wills" of God.

To live under the Old Covenant is to live under a two-sided, conditional covenant. If a person fulfills the requirements of the Law, they will be blessed. But if they disobey or fail, they come under a curse, resulting in punishment.

In Galatians 3:10–11, quoting from Deuteronomy 27:26 and Habakkuk 2:4, Paul wrote:

For as many as are of the works of the Law are under a curse; for it is written, "Cursed is everyone who does not abide by *all* things written in the book of the Law, to perform them." Now that no one is justified by the Law is evident; for, "The righteous man shall live by faith." (emphasis mine)

It is clear from these passages that if a person does not abide by everything written in the Law, he is cursed. To be more specific, that means that every moment of every day, seven days a week, fifty-two weeks of every year, for as many years as a person lives, that person needs to perfectly obey everything in the Law or else he will fall under a curse.

There are three major problems with the Old Covenant, which was written on cold, hard tablets of stone. First, it is impossible to keep. Second, it could not justify a person before God (only by faith can one be justified). Third and finally, it could not forgive sins.

> For the Law, having a shadow of the good things to come and not the very image of things, can *never*, with these same sacrifices which they offer continually year by year, make those who approach perfect. (Hebrews 10:1, emphasis mine)

> For it is impossible for the blood of bulls and goats to take away sins. (Hebrews 10:4)

The New Covenant, however, is a covenant God makes with every believer. He promises that he will write his laws upon our hearts.

> "Behold, days are coming," declares the Lord, "when I will make a new covenant with the house of Israel and with the house of Judah, not like the covenant which I made with their fathers in the day I took them by the hand to bring them out of the land of Egypt, my covenant which they broke, although I was a husband to them," declares the Lord. "But this is the covenant which I will make with the house of Israel after those days," declares the Lord, "I will put my law within them and on their heart I will write it, and I will be their God and they shall be my people. They will not teach again, each man his neighbor and each man his brother, saying, 'Know the Lord,' for they will all know me, from the least of them to the greatest of them," declares the Lord, "for I will forgive their iniquity, and their sin I will remember no more." (Jeremiah 31:31–34)

Unlike the Old Covenant, the New Covenant is a unilateral agreement. It is one-sided. There are no conditions we are required to keep. There are no "ifs." God doesn't promise to bless us "if." It is an unconditional covenant. There are only "I wills."

As we see them in Jeremiah 31, here are the three "I wills" of the New Covenant:

- "I will put my laws within you and write them on your hearts."
- "I will be your God, and you will be my people."
- "I will forgive your iniquity and your sin I will remember no more."

This is truly good news to one who knows his own weaknesses—and wonderful news to anyone who has ever tried living under the Law! If you have been there, you know how important it is to have a new covenant without any ifs. Our flesh cannot cope with any ifs. This is a covenant of pure grace.

THOUGHTS/PRAYERS

Lord, kiss me with the revelation that the young maiden received when she heard from her beloved his promise to exchange her beads for his necklace. Thank you that you have promised that, through the transforming work of the Holy Spirit, I will be made into the person you want me to be. Thank you that for anything I need, you have made the provision. Let me see you and know you as the God of the "I will."

Now the God of peace, who brought up from the dead the great Shepherd of the sheep through the blood of the eternal covenant, even Jesus our Lord, *equip* you in every good thing to do his will, *working in us* that which is pleasing in his sight, through Jesus Christ, to whom be the glory forever and ever. Amen. (Hebrews 13:20, emphasis mine)

Death and Resurrection

SONG OF SONGS, CHAPTER 1

"My beloved is to me a pouch of myrrh
Which lies all night between my breasts.
My beloved is to me a cluster of henna blossoms
In the vineyards of Engedi."

SONG OF SONGS 1:13–14

Days later, I decided to visit the bazaar of a larger village not far from my home. I brought some rounds of goat cheese with me to barter with the vendors.

As I roamed around the marketplace, all that I could think about was the king. I passed by one of the vendor's booths, and suddenly my senses were arrested by an aromatic scent which I could not at first identify. Looking around for the origin of this intoxicating perfume, I came to a table filled with many unusually shaped bottles of oils and perfumes amidst colorful boxes of different sizes, decorated with jewels. Behind the ancient table was a merchant I had never seen before, an aged man with thin, scraggly gray hair and a toothless smile.

"I sense something unique that is coming forth from your table," I said to the man.

Looking up, his eyes lit up as though he recognized me. "Are you the young maiden?" he asked. He saw that I did not immediately understand, so he continued, "Are you the one with whom it is rumored that King Solomon has fallen in love?"

I did not answer. I felt protective about disclosing my relationship to the king.

When he saw that I was not going to respond, he continued. "Let me tell you about this collection of herbs, spices, and oils." With that, he began going from box to box, opening wide the lids. One by one, with his short, stocky arms, he lifted them up close to my nose for me to smell.

Coming to the frankincense, the old man said, "This prized spice has journeyed from a faraway place in the east by way of a caravan, on the backs of donkeys and camels. If you were to give me an ounce of gold, I could only give you a pinch of frankincense. Its value lies in its exotic smell. In its purest form, this is the frankincense that Jehovah commanded Moses to use to make the incense that was to be burned before the Lord in the tabernacle's most holy place. This is a precious spice indeed."

I took a light sniff of the frankincense. Its fragrance was truly beautiful, but it was not what I had smelled. "Could it be something else?" I asked.

"Yes," said the old man, with a sly smile. "I believe what your sensitive sense of smell has detected is myrrh. Myrrh is the precious ingredient that, when mixed with oil and other spices in proportions known only to the priests, is used in making the holy anointing oil by which kings and the high priest are anointed."

Reaching for one of his boxes, he pulled from it a small pouch which was fastened to a thin leather strap. His bushy eyebrows raised, and his eyes grew wide as he held it up before me.

"This myrrh comes from a reddish-brown resin within the tree. We must cut the tree open in order to draw forth this gummy sap. Then it hardens into small crystals. Once the crystals, called tears, are dry, they can be set on fire. Then the slow-burning substance emits the most pleasing fragrance. Myrrh is often used at funerals to chase away the scent of death. Sometimes it is crushed and added to oil to preserve and spread upon the bodies of the dead."

"This is the smell I recognized!" I said, my voice exposing my excitement. "It is the smell that I adore when I am near…"

But then I stopped short.

The old man resumed, "Myrrh is so rare and costly that it can be used in exchange for money. High-quality myrrh can be up to five times more expensive than frankincense! Strangely enough, the taste of it is quite bitter, although its smell is incomparable. Sometimes those who are dying or greatly afflicted ask for myrrh to be mixed with wine in order to dull their pain."

"How long does the beautiful aroma coming from this pouch last?" I asked him.

"That depends," he said. "When it is left alone, you might believe that it has lost its aroma, but if it comes into touch with warmth, it will once more ignite in its fragrance."

I was afraid to ask the man the value of the small pouch, fearing that it would be far too expensive for me to afford. But finally, I mustered the courage. "How much goat cheese would you take in exchange for the pouch?" I inquired.

"Keep your cheese," he said, shaking his head. "I know who you are. Consider this a special gift for a special lady. Someday you will have the means with which to repay me. I would only ask that you visit me again the next time you are in this village, and that you do not forget me."

"Oh, thank you!" I exclaimed as he handed me the pouch and I squeezed it tightly in my hands. "I will return. And I certainly will not forget you!"

Pressing deeper into the bustling market, I heard a cry from another vendor, "Flowers! Henna blossoms from Engedi. Flowers, anyone?" Turning toward the source of the shouting, I saw an aging, poorly clad woman limping through the crowd of shoppers, waving a bouquet of branchy clusters of white, four-petaled henna flowers. Catching up with the woman, I tapped her on the shoulder, and she turned to face me.

"May I see your flowers?" I asked.

Long ago, I had been to that lush oasis at Engedi in the scorching desert by the edge of the Dead Sea. As I admired the flowers, I remembered the waterfall that spills down the steep, brown cliffs into the large pool where travelers go to draw water and bathe. I recalled the name *Engedi* and its meaning: "the Fountain of the Lamb." I reminisced upon the vineyards there, surrounded and protected by the thorny, bushy henna hedges, which grow in a place where no one would expect such life and such fragrance. The memory brought me great pleasure.

"I will take that bouquet of henna flowers," I told the lady as I meted a round of cheese in exchange for the flowers.

After I had returned to my home that night, I lay down on my straw mat to retire for the evening. I clutched the little satchel of myrrh which hung between my breasts and placed it directly over my heart. The warmth of my body, combined with the myrrh, kindled a pleasing scent that gently wafted into the air. *It was just like the old man promised.*

Looking over at the bouquet of henna flowers next to me, the sweet, fragrant aroma from its blossoms suddenly engulfed my senses. Deeply content, I thought, *What a pleasing combination this is; one fragrance associated with death and another with life which comes out of death.* As my eyes closed and I mused on this apparent paradox, my thoughts gradually returned to the king, and I drifted off into a deep and peaceful sleep.

POINTS TO CONSIDER

Myrrh comes from a variety of spindly, unattractive trees that grow in the dry, arid climate of the Middle East. These trees are reminiscent of Christ, who, as Isaiah wrote:

...grew up before Him like a tender shoot, and like a root out of parched ground; He has no stately form or majesty that we should look upon Him, nor appearance that we should be attracted to Him. He was despised and forsaken of men, a man of sorrows and acquainted with grief; and like one from whom men hid their face He was despised, and we did not esteem Him." (Isaiah 53: 2–3)

Myrrh was the primary ingredient used in making the holy anointing oil (Exodus 30: 22–25), while frankincense was used to make the incense which was burned before the Lord (Exodus 30:34–37).

On three occasions, myrrh is used in the New Testament in connection with Jesus. In each case, it symbolically represents suffering and death.

- The first time myrrh appears is when the magi come from the east bearing their treasures of gold, frankincense, and myrrh to honor the infant king in Matthew 2:11. They knew that gifts honoring a king must be of rare quality and great value. As they worshiped Christ, the gift of myrrh with which they honored him represented the suffering he would embrace both in life and ultimately in death, as he bore in his body the sins of the whole world. Symbolically, their gifts acknowledged that he was God (gold), that he would be our High Priest who intercedes for us (frankincense), and that he was our Savior (myrrh).
- The next time myrrh is mentioned is when it is mixed with wine and offered to Christ as he hangs on the tree in Mark 15:23. He refused to drink the numbing beverage, so as in no way to dilute the full cup of the wrath of God which he drank on our behalf.
- Finally, myrrh appears again in John 19:39 when Nicodemus "brought a mixture of myrrh and aloes, about a hundred pounds" to embalm Christ's body. Normally, only about a pound of myrrh was used in the Hebrew funeral preparations. But out of the greatest respect for him whom Pilate called "King of the Jews," Nicodemus brought an excessive amount of myrrh and aloes to prepare his body for burial.

The sachet of myrrh that hung from the maiden's neck and lay between her breasts represents, for the believer, a deep, heartfelt appreciation for the suffering and death of Christ.

Consider all that Christ took to the grave with him when he died for you on that tree:

- All of your individual sins (Hebrews 7:26-27)
- Sin—your old "self" and sinful nature (Romans 6:6–7)
- Your flesh (Galatians 5:24)
- "You" (Galatians 2:20)
- The Law (Ephesians 2:13–16)
- The world (Galatians 6:14)
- All accusations against you (Colossians 2:14)
- The rulers and authorities in heavenly places (Colossians 2:15)
- Satan (Hebrews 2:14)
- Death (1 Corinthians 15:16)

After three days, Christ arose. But he was not alone. You were raised with him! All of those negative things were left in the tomb.

> If then you were raised with Christ, seek those things which are above, where Christ is, sitting at the right hand of God. Set your mind on things above, not on things on the earth. For you died and your life is hidden with Christ in God. When Christ, who is our life appears, then you also will appear with him in glory. (Colossians 3:1–4)

Not only was the king as a pouch of myrrh to the maiden, but he was also as a bouquet of henna blossoms in the vineyards of Engedi. Henna produces whitish, fragrant flowers that are used in making perfume. It was near Engedi that David found refuge at "the Fountain of the Lamb" and was delivered from Saul and an army of three thousand men. He emerged victorious from the recesses of a cave and was recognized by Saul as the one whom God had made king and to whom he had given the kingdom (1 Samuel 24).

The henna blossoms represent the resurrection life of Christ. Significantly, in the Song of Songs, myrrh is mentioned before henna. Loss must always precede gain. Death always precedes resurrection.

Like Aaron's rod that budded in the wilderness, blossoms speak of the new life that sprouts from what is apparently dead wood. This beautiful bouquet of henna blossoms, taken from the barren surroundings of a lifeless desert, tell of Christ's resurrection life. It is a life that conquers death and is now living and reigning in you!

May the smell of the myrrh and the scent of the henna blossoms fill your senses today as you contemplate the simple gospel message of Christ's death and resurrection.

For I delivered to you first of all that which I also received: that Christ died for our sins according to the Scriptures, and that he was buried, and that He rose again the third day according to the Scriptures. (1 Corinthians 15:3–4)

A Foretaste of Rest and Union

SONG OF SONGS, CHAPTER 1

"How beautiful you are, my darling,
How beautiful you are!
Your eyes are like doves."

"How handsome you are, my beloved,
And so pleasant!"

"Indeed, our couch is luxuriant!
The beams of our houses are cedars,
Our rafters, cypresses."

SONG OF SONGS 1:15–17

The following day, there came a knock on the maiden's door. Opening it, she saw that it was one of the king's servants.

"A message from the king," the young man said, as he handed her a petite scroll.

She opened and read it. "Yes," she said with a smile. "Tell the king that I will gladly see him tomorrow."

"I will be here to pick you up at an hour past sunrise and take you to him," the servant responded.

"Tell him I will be ready and waiting," she replied.

⁓ ⁓ ⁓

As on other occasions when the maiden and I had met, this meeting was to be one away from the city. In our short courtship, I had discovered that she too loved nature and the outdoors. With the stress and responsibilities that accompanied my position as king over Israel, I always looked forward to taking her away to someplace new, out in the open air where we could be alone together, relax, and talk.

This time, our rendezvous was in the hill country, in a grassy meadow above the tree line. Surrounding the meadow was a forest filled with cedar, fir, and cypress trees. Four chariots, manned with soldiers and servants, accompanied the maiden and me. We rode as far as the road would take us, then got out and hiked up to a small bluff with a panoramic view overlooking the valley below. Leaving the soldiers and servants behind with the chariots, the maiden and I walked ahead a short distance, hand in hand, and found a comfortable patch of grass on which to sit down.

I did most of the talking. Perhaps it was not very romantic of me, but our conversation turned into a lesson in botany and dendrology. With nature itself as our classroom, I pointed out to her all the different varieties of surrounding trees, plants, and even birds, identifying them all by name. She listened with true interest, making me love her all the more!

Suddenly, interrupting my lecture, we heard the distinct sound of doves cooing. Turning our heads in the direction of their beautiful melody, we spotted two sitting on the branch of a nearby cypress. It seemed as if they were singing to us! I turned to my love and said, "You are so beautiful, my darling. Your dark eyes are like the eyes of those innocent doves that entertain us with their song."

"Is it any wonder, my king, that when I am with you my eyes, like those of the dove, can fix upon only one object at a time? I choose to fix them upon you," she responded. "You are so handsome, my beloved, and so pleasant."

"It is curious that you call me 'my beloved,'" I told her, "for that is a name that another calls me as well."

Her face abruptly displayed concern.

I chuckled. "Do not worry, my darling, for I will tell you a secret that few people know. When I was born, my father named me *Solomon,* a name which means 'peace.' But I was given a second name as well. You see, God spoke through the prophet Nathan, saying, 'Tell David that I have a special love for this son who has been born to you. I will call him *Jedidiah,* which means 'beloved of the Lord.'"

"How beautiful!" she exclaimed. "A secret name from the Almighty. If the one who created the heavens and this earth calls you his beloved, I will gladly do so as well!"

"There is something more I would like you to know of me," I said. "Before I was even born, the God of Israel appeared to my father, King David, and told him that I, his son, would build a great house for our God. My father became almost obsessed with collecting material for that house from the spoils of war and the freewill offerings of the people. He even contributed a fortune from his own treasury. Gold, silver, bronze, precious stones, timber, and fabrics were amassed, so much that it is difficult to imagine. His passion burned to build this house. The Almighty even gave to him the exact pattern by which to build it, in all its detail—but I was the one appointed to the task of building it. For you see, my father was a man of war, and blood was on his hands. Therefore, he was not allowed to build it.

"As glorious as this building will be, I sometimes ask myself, 'What thing of beauty can man build compared to the Creator?' As our eyes feast on all that surrounds us here, I cannot help but wonder: How could this remarkable architect and designer of the whole world ever contain himself in a house made by human hands? The heavens are his throne and the earth is his footstool. Heaven, even the highest heaven, cannot contain him!

"What's more," I continued, "I will tell you something else. This same God made another promise to my father, saying, 'Behold, a son will be born to you, who shall be a man of rest. I will give him rest from all his enemies on every side; for his name shall be Solomon, and I will give peace and quiet to Israel all of his days.' He also said that he 'would establish the throne of my kingdom over Israel forever.' Although my father was a man of war, there would be rest and peace during my reign. Rest and peace. Is that not what every person longs for?"

"Yes," she responded. "It is the desire of every soul. Truly, the two names suit you well. If I could but speak for all within your kingdom, I could rightly say that to be with you is to be with the one who is beloved of God, and in your presence there is rest and peace indeed."

"For as long as we live together, it will be so," I replied.

With that, we both reclined on our bed of tall, fragrant grass. Resting comfortably and at peace under the overhanging boughs of the trees, we gazed heavenward at the clear blue sky. Silently, we absorbed the beauty. "Indeed, our couch is luxuriant!" I said. "Although the God of Israel may choose to inhabit a house made of stone, the beams of our houses are cedars; our rafters, cypresses."

She was quiet a moment, then inquired in a voice tinged with surprise. "Did you say *our* couch, *our* houses, and *our* rafters, my king?"

"Yes, my love," I told her. "You heard me correctly. When you have become my wife, I want to share everything in my kingdom with you. It shall *all* be *ours!*"

POINTS TO CONSIDER

The importance of learning to rest "in Christ" cannot be overstated. This rest is at the heart of all spiritual fruitfulness.

From the very beginning, God has always wanted man to enter into rest with him. On the sixth day of creation, he created the man and the woman. On the seventh day, God rested. He commanded the man and woman to "be fruitful and multiply, fill the earth, and subdue it; and rule over the fish of the sea and the birds of the sky and over every living thing that moves on the earth" (Genesis 1:28), but before they could lift even one finger to work, they woke up on the seventh day—God's day of rest! Adam and Eve's first day was not a day of work, but a day of resting with God.

Moses, in giving the Law, instructed the Israelites to take one day a week to rest from their labors. Every seventh month, he had them observe a feast to remember that they could rest and trust in the Lord. Every seventh year, God told them to take a whole year off to rest and watch him provide for them:

> You shall sow your land for six years and gather in its yield, but on the seventh year you shall let it rest and lie fallow so that the needy of your people may eat; and whatever they leave the beast of the field may eat. You are to do the same with your vineyard and your olive grove. (Exodus 23:10–11)

> But if you say, "What are we going to eat on the seventh year if we do not sow or gather in our crops?" Then I will so order My blessing for you in the sixth year that it will bring forth crop for three years. (Leviticus 25:20–22)

During the seventh year, or the "sabbatical year," the people could hunt and fish, care for their flocks, repair their homes, make clothing, and teach one another and their children the ways of God, but God wanted them to let the land rest, and he promised to provide for them.

God knew their hearts, as he does yours! He wanted to demonstrate his love for them, and in the same way, he wants to demonstrate his love for you. But he knew that it would require an act of faith for his people to believe that he would actually provide even if they didn't work to plant their crops or tend to their vineyards and trees. So what did he do? He made a promise that in the sixth year, to make up for that seventh year when the ground would lie fallow, he would provide three times the amount of crops to carry them through.

Imagine if you were one of the Israelites living in the land of Canaan. On the plot of land given you for your inheritance, you had a few olive trees or some grapevines or a field of wheat. You knew what a normal year's yield was like. But now, envision that your olive trees, your grapevines, or your field of wheat produced three times its normal amount in a single year! Each day before harvest, you would walk out to see your trees or your vines getting more and more heavy laden with fruit, to the point where the branches were near to snapping, while your rows of wheat were getting thicker and taller than anything you had ever seen before!

But the Israelites never experienced God's bountiful promise. During the whole period of the kings, God's people kept working without taking a year off. Seventy sabbatical years went by. They were not counting, but God was! Finally, after four hundred and ninety years had passed—seventy sabbatical years of not honoring the Lord—God sent them into captivity to Babylon for seventy years, one year for each sabbatical year they had neglected to rest in him and trust his provision (2 Chronicles 36:20–21).

The land of Canaan was the Israelites' heritage. It was a rich land, flowing with milk and honey. Joshua led them into the land and divided it up among the twelve tribes. They were to work the land, take all of their sustenance from the land, and enjoy the land. But due to their neglect of honoring the sabbatical year prescribed by God, they lost it and were sent into captivity in Babylon (which literally means "confusion") for seventy years.

The spiritual analogy is this: When we became Christians, Christ came into our spirits to live. He is in us, and we are "in him." We have all of him. Our inheritance is not a physical land. Our inheritance is Christ, and we can live in this wonderful Christ, partake of his divine nature, and enjoy all spiritual blessings in the heavenly places in him as we learn to rest and abide in him. But sometimes, due to unfaithfulness, we may lose the experience of drawing our strength and resources from him and enjoying his blessings. That will one day lead to our waking up and finding ourselves in a state of confusion and spiritual captivity.

When this happens, in our desire to come back to the Lord and find his presence once again, the natural reaction is to backtrack to see if we can identify the cause of our departure or perceived separation from him. Was it a gradual slipping away? Was it an immoral act? Was it lying, cheating, stealing, coveting, worldliness, pride, uncontrolled outbursts of anger, speaking evil of another brother or sister, or even outright rebellion? Did we turn away because God disappointed us or didn't live up to our expectations of who we imagined him to be? Any one of these or other sins could have brought on our break in fellowship with him. But we must ask ourselves, is there a more basic common denominator, a shared place of departure, a root sin that is the reason we, like the Old and New Testament saints, stray into spiritual captivity?

In spiritual terms, the Old Testament saints' refusal to honor the sabbatical years and trust in God's provision resulted in their captivity. For the Christian, it is no different. Captivity is the result of failing to rest in Christ and trust his abundant provision.

"Abide in me and I in you." (John 15:4)

"Come unto me all you who are weary and heavy laden and I will give you rest." (Matthew 11:25)

As Solomon and the maiden lay resting together, she learned that all that was his also belonged to her. Resting is the starting place of all spiritual fruitfulness.

THOUGHTS/PRAYERS

Allow Christ to be your Sabbath rest today. Rest in union with him, looking up into the heavens and watching as he abundantly provides for all your needs!

The Banqueting Hall

Song of Songs, Chapter 2
"I am the rose of Sharon,
The lily of the valleys."

"Like a lily among the thorns,
So is my darling among the maidens."

"Like an apple tree among the trees of the forest,
So is my beloved among the young men
In his shade I took great delight and sat down,
And his fruit was sweet to my taste.
He has brought me to his banquet hall,
And his banner over me is love.
Sustain me with raisin cakes,
Refresh me with apples,
Because I am lovesick.
Let his left hand be under my head
And his right hand embrace me."

SONG OF SONGS 2:1–6

Our times together, my maiden's and mine, became more frequent. Occasionally I would come for her myself. At other times I would send one of my servants to bring her to the palace or to meet me at some designated location. One day, I asked her to prepare for a longer trip to visit my winter home in Lebanon. The journey would take several days.

We set out with a large entourage accompanying us—soldiers, servants, cooks, guards, guests, singers, and musicians. I sent some of them ahead to announce our arrival and to prepare for our coming. When we finally arrived at the winter palace, it was dusk on the twelfth day, just in time for the evening meal. The maiden and I dismounted from my chariot and walked together across the spacious courtyard of large, hewn stones, which led to the banqueting hall. As we approached the hall, she looked up in wonder at the great cedar pillars supporting and surrounding it.

"At last we are here, my dear," I said. "Inside, you will meet foreign dignitaries and visitors, my royal court, along with those who regularly join me at my table. I want them to see you. I want to put you on display. You will be seated next to me at the head of the table, in the shade of my right hand, so that all will know that you are my true love."

"I feel overwhelmed," she responded. "What an honor this is for me, my king. But I must confess, I am just an ordinary wildflower, like a rose of Sharon or a lily from the valley. Why me? I deserve nothing like this."

"Perhaps a lily," I replied quickly, "but to me, you are like a lily among thorns— so tender, so soft, so vulnerable, and so beautiful. All the other maidens of the land, by comparison, are but thistles when you are found in their midst."

With a slight laugh, she quickly returned the compliment. "And to me, my king, you are truly like an apple tree among the trees of the forest!"

As we neared the entrance way of great hall, she gasped. "This is so beautiful!" Amazement and wonder filled her eyes.

"I wanted this to be a place of feasting for all the senses—all you see, all you taste, all you touch, all you hear, and all you smell," I said.

On cue, guards appeared and opened the great doors. As we stepped inside, the bugles blared, announcing our entrance. Instantly our senses were filled with the fresh scent of cedar. The luxurious wood was everywhere, forming the floors, the paneling, the artistic window frames, and the pillars. She gazed around in awe at the walls, and then at the three rows of windows on opposite sides of the hall, symmetrically facing one another and allowing the sun to fall upon the banqueting table.

Hanging high on the walls were large shields. I saw her eyes fasten on the shields, and I said, "Those shields you are looking at, my darling, are among two hundred I had made—each one created from six hundred shekels of beaten gold. The smaller ones are from among the two hundred that were made of three hundred shekels of beaten gold each. I want all who enter this place—friends and potential enemies alike—to know how fiercely I am committed to protecting all that is within my kingdom." Her eyes met mine, and I smiled. "That includes you, my love! These shields will take on an even more significant meaning for you in the days ahead."

As we entered the hall, all eyes were upon us. I was accustomed to this attention, but she was not, and I saw her mingled discomfort and pleasure. We were escorted to our seats and sat down at the head of the long banqueting table, which also was made of cedar. It was surrounded with guests and crowded with lush, succulent dishes. Over the very place where we sat was a large banner that I had made especially for this occasion. It was woven in beautiful white linen and gold. Inscribed on the banner was but one solitary word: "Love."

Standing at attention behind the guests were hundreds of handsome, well-groomed waiters dressed in brilliant, colorful clothing. Each one was trained to anticipate the needs of the banqueters and treat them like royalty. As my love stared down the lengthy table, I commented on the abundant provisions. "Each day this table is filled with delicacies made from three hundred bushels of fine flour and six hundred bushels of meal. The meat includes the choice cuts from ten fat oxen, twenty pasture-fed oxen, and a hundred sheep, not to mention deer, gazelles, roebucks, and fattened fowl."

"And there," she pointed with excitement, "I see a large platter of raisin cakes. They look delicious! How did you know they were among my favorite treats?"

"My chefs have a way of knowing," I responded with a smile.

The drinking cups before us were made of gold. My cupbearer carefully poured the wine, sampled it, and then handed one chalice to me and one to my love.

I stood up, and the room immediately became quiet. I raised my cup in honor of my special guest. "Join me, friends and guests, in honoring this beautiful maiden who sits beside me today. With these chalices of gold, we toast this lady with the finest of wine. A silver chalice, or anything of lesser value, would not do, for silver is as common in my kingdom as the stones in Jerusalem. Only a golden chalice is worthy of such a one as this!"

I had once again succeeded in embarrassing her with my lavish praise. She blushed as all who sat at the table raised their glasses, and after a thunderous cheer, partook of the fruit of the vine.

We sat down. She picked up a piece of fruit from the bowl sitting next to my arm and held it before my eyes. "This apple is one of my favorite fruits," she said. "I told you earlier that you were like an apple tree among the forest. This is how you stand out to me among all the young men. There is none like you! With each bite of this fruit, I will be refreshed with thoughts only of you!"

When the feast finally ended, we were the last ones sitting at the table. The other guests had long since gone, and the remaining food and dishes had been taken away. I ordered my servants to bring a large candlestick and place it beside us so that we could continue to talk in the glimmer of its light.

As it was getting late and time for us to retire, I said to her, "I confess that I am as content as I can be—not only from the great banquet, nor from being in the company of all the guests that were here. My joy is made full just by being with you. I do, however, have one last thing to ask of you. I would like to know, has this night been all that you had hoped for and expected it to be?"

"My joy and contentment overflow," she responded. "The love you show to me exceeds anything I could ever have envisioned! Surely, I have taken in too much this night. As some become sick by taking in too much food and strong drink, so I am sick with love!"

We clasped hands.

"You asked if this night had been all that I had hoped for, and I will answer your question truthfully," she continued. She drew close to me, so close that our faces almost touched. She looked into my eyes and whispered, "Throughout this night, romantic thoughts of being alone with you have been dancing through my head. Although I know that this is not the time or the hour, the only joy left unfulfilled is the thought of you putting your left hand under my head, and your right hand embracing me as you give me *all* of your love!"

"Can you not see the same desire in my own eyes? It is fueled by those same thoughts that blaze like wildfire within me!" I replied in earnest. "I have lived with this burning passion for you since the day I first saw you in the field. I assure you, my love, that the day will come, and come soon, when our deepest longings will no longer need to be restrained, when no part of love will need to be held back, when it will all be spent. I pledge that to you this night, with this kiss."

With that, our eyes closed, and our lips joined in tender union. I savored the long, delicious kiss, as did she.

When our lips finally parted, I said to her, "This is only a foretaste, my love, of what is to come."

"Yes," she echoed, with a smile.

Reluctantly, we arose from the table. We exited the banqueting hall holding hands as I escorted her to the adjoining residence. There we were met by some of the daughters of Jerusalem who cared for the residence and for all of my guests.

Bidding her goodnight, I turned to the other young ladies and said, "Escort the maiden to the room that has been prepared for her. Let her rest as long as she likes. When she awakes, tend to her every need. I charge you, O daughters, by the gazelles, or by the hinds of the field, that you do not arouse or awaken my love until she pleases."

POINTS TO CONSIDER

A description of the architecture of Solomon's palaces is found in 1 Kings 7:1–12, the shields in 2 Chronicles 9:13–16, the drinking vessels of gold in 2 Chronicles 9:20, and the daily provision at his table in 1 Kings 4:22–23.

Earlier, the king brought the maiden to see his bedchamber. Now, he brings her to his banqueting hall. The spiritual message here is that the Lord not only wants to bring us to a place of rest and intimacy, but to a place where we can learn to feast upon him and enjoy him as our food.

In the garden of Eden, God first presented himself to man as food, as represented by the Tree of Life.

Jesus came as the fulfillment of what that tree represented. "I have come that you might have life [God's life; eternal, uncreated life; the highest life in the universe; the very life that God lives by], and that you might have *that life* in abundance" (John 10:10, emphasis mine).

- Jesus presented himself to us as:
- Bread that is alive (John 6:51)
- Water that is alive (John 4:10)
- Real food and real drink (John 6:55; Colossians 2:16–17)
- The reality behind all the Old Testament feasts (Colossians 2:16–17)

To learn to eat of him is not only important, but a necessity.

Man shall not live on bread alone, but on every word that proceeds out of the mouth of God. (Matthew 4:4)

O taste and see that the Lord is good. (Psalm 34:8)

To take Christ as food is to learn to turn within, to where he lives within our spirits, and draw our strength from him. To know him as our drink is to know him as the one who provides refreshment to our souls, like a cool glass of water. Eating and drinking of Christ is at the very heart of God's eternal purpose for man.

In the New Jerusalem described in Revelation 21 and 22, the whole city (which is the bride of Christ) is nourished and fed from the Tree of Life and watered by the river of the water of life that flows freely from the throne of God and of the Lamb (Revelation 22:1–3). Christ now dwells within us, in our spirits (1 Corinthians 6:17); his Spirit joined with our spirits.

The words he speaks within us are spirit and are life (John 6:63).

Not only do we eat of him "in spirit," but we worship him "in spirit and in truth" (or "in spirit and in reality"—John 4:23–24).

We must learn, as this maiden symbolizes, to let Christ lead us into his banqueting hall. As we feed on him and enjoy him, we discover that surely his banner over us is love!

THOUGHTS/PRAYERS

Lord Jesus, you are true food and you are true drink. I need to eat and drink of you every day. Bring me to your banqueting table now. I want to enjoy being in your presence, feasting on you and delighting in you. Be my daily bread. Be my living water. I worship you, Lord, and thank you for your love!

The Wall

SONG OF SONGS, CHAPTER 2

"I adjure you, O daughters of Jerusalem,
By the gazelles or by the hinds of the field,
That you do not arouse or awaken my love
Until she pleases."

"Listen! My beloved!
Behold, he is coming,
Climbing on the mountains,
Leaping on the hills!
My beloved is like a gazelle or a young stag.
Behold, he is standing behind our wall,
He is looking through the windows,
He is peering through the lattice.
My beloved responded and said to me,
'Arise, my darling, my beautiful one,
And come along.
For behold, the winter is past,
The rain is over and gone.
The flowers have already appeared in the land;
The time has arrived for pruning the vines,
And the voice of the turtledove has been heard in our land.
The fig tree has ripened its figs,
And the vines in blossom have given forth their fragrance.
Arise, my darling, my beautiful one,
And come along!'"

SONG OF SONGS 2:7–19

Days passed, and I became quite comfortable in my new surroundings. Maid-servants waited upon me day and night. A lavish wardrobe was provided for me. In my leisure moments, I took great pleasure in listening to the singing of the Levite choir and the daily music supplied by the skilled musicians. The breads, the meats, the sauces, the fruits which were available at every meal, and in such abundance, were beyond anything I had ever imagined existed.

One morning, as one of the daughters of Jerusalem was pouring water for my bath, I inquired of her, "Where is my beloved?"

"He is not here. He has gone to the mountains to inspect the timbers that are being gathered and will be used in the temple in Jerusalem," was the reply.

"Not here?" I said in astonishment. "How can this be? I thought he would always be here with me."

How long he had been gone, I did not know. It could have been a few days—maybe more. Strange as it may seem, in his absence I had grown rather content, absorbed by all the new surroundings. But suddenly, I felt the sharp pang of remorse. *How foolish of me,* I thought. *Have I actually neglected the king as I have been enjoying all of the benefits he has bestowed upon me? Have I taken him for granted? How horribly ungrateful he must think I am!*

In the warmth and protection I had known within the king's winter palace, I had not been aware of the creeping winter within my own heart.

Later that day, I sat on the edge of my bed in the opulent chamber which had become my temporary residence, talking with an attendant. By now, I had become despondent and very anxious about the king's whereabouts, not knowing when he would return. I even began to wonder if maybe his love for me had grown cold.

Then, unexpectedly, I heard a faint shout coming from outside in the distance. Abruptly, I stood up and raced to the window. "Listen!" I exclaimed to my companion. "It is my beloved! I see him! Behold he is coming, climbing on the mountains, leaping on the hills. Look at him! He looks so free, so agile, as a gazelle or a young stag bounding upon the rocks!"

He disappeared from my sight momentarily. Hopeful to see him once more, I continued gazing out the window until he might appear again. There he was! This time he was much closer. Now he was behind a stone wall, which separated the palace from the field beyond, not too far in the distance. He was standing on his tiptoes—even straining—to look in my window and through the latticework to see if I was there.

"I am here, Solomon!" I cried, although I did not know if he could hear me. "I am here!"

In a strong, bellowing voice, I heard him shout again, saying, "Arise, my darling, my beautiful one, and come with me! The winter is past, and the rains have come and gone. The flowers have appeared in the land! The singing of birds and the cooing of the turtledoves fills the air! I will take you with me to the vineyards, and we will play among them while their vines give forth their fragrances. We will pick figs, and from there we will explore the rocky places and find some secret place within the cliffs. Come, my shy dove! Come out in the open and go with me!"

POINTS TO CONSIDER

In this passage, the maiden's royal lover continues his pursuit, drawing her, beckoning her to come away with him. Previously, she rested with him on their bed of green, gazing heavenward. Then she was escorted by him into his banqueting hall (literally, "the house of wine"), where his banner over her was love. Now he comes to her again, revealing himself as one climbing on the mountains and leaping upon the hills.

The imagery here is striking. He was on the mountains, but she was behind a wall. He was free, but she was enclosed. He was leaping, but she was stationary. Undaunted by the mountains (the big problems in life) and the hills (the smaller obstacles and difficulties), he leapt and triumphed over them. Meanwhile, the maiden would have loved to be with him where he was, but she had retreated. A wall now separated them. And as we discover as we read on, she was not able to respond to his call.

The maiden's initial stage of love is one full of discovery, revelation, and new encounters with her beloved. But in it, there is also a winter season. During the winter season, she moves from experiencing the presence of her beloved more and more to experiencing him less and less. She also loses the sense that, in the king's eyes, she is still his most beautiful one. Although on the one hand she wants to be with him, on the other, she has withdrawn behind a wall.

For the believer, the Lord's visitations, in the words of Madame Guyon, may be not only "pledges of his love, but tokens of his departure."

In the beginning, it was the king's displays of affection that drew the maiden and caused her to love him. But would she still love him in the absence of those exhibits of affection?

In our spiritual immaturity, we can sometimes become addicted to the wonderful feelings that are aroused when the Lord gives us the sense of his intoxicating presence. But during the winter seasons, when we are tested, will we continue to love and follow the Lord even if we are not experiencing him or feeling the nearness of his presence? Do we love him for those moments of ecstasy when we feel his touch?

Or do we love him for who he is, regardless of whether or not we are experiencing his gifts and benefits? Stripped of feeling, can we remain steadfast and demonstrate our love for him, even if it is by faith alone?

Although we may know that there is freedom in Christ, isn't it true that sometimes we find ourselves behind some kind of wall and not living in that freedom?

In the Christian experience, that wall can be built of a variety of things.

In some cases, there are times in our spiritual journey after we have had a wonderful encounter with the Lord—like being together with him on "our couch" or feasting with him in his banqueting hall—when we find a place of contentment from which we do not want to move on. It is not uncommon to set up camp at the altar of one spiritual experience and refuse to move on to another. But doing so denies the Giver of all spiritual blessings the opportunity to lead us out of our comfort zones and into new frontiers of spiritual discovery.

Any spiritual experience can turn into an idol when we shift from seeking the Lord himself to focusing on something else. It could be the gifts of the Spirit. It could be the love of speaking before crowds. It could be the church. It could be some pet doctrine or a variety of other things. Whatever it is, whenever we seek something other than Christ or elevate something else to the place that he alone should occupy, he will eventually remove the sense of his presence from us, and we will find ourselves on our own bed, with a wall between us and him.

The wall of separation can also take the form of our own system of theology. It may be some doctrine that we have constructed and lean upon instead of leaning upon Christ himself. We see this in the life of Simon Peter. His "theology" was shattered over and over again so that Christ could deliver him and become his all. Take, for example, the time on the Mount of Transfiguration when Peter saw Christ appear in glory, talking with Moses and Elijah. Peter wanted to build three tabernacles—one for each one of them. In Peter's theology, he saw them all as equals: Christ, Moses (representing the Law), and Elijah (representing the prophets). But then came the voice from heaven: "This is my beloved Son, with whom I am well pleased; listen to him!" And looking up, Peter and the others saw no one but Jesus alone.

In the Old Testament, if a person wanted to know what he could eat or how much work he could do on a Sabbath, he would go to the book of the Law to find the answer. If someone wanted to know whether or not to marry a particular man or woman or take a trip, he or she would go to a prophet who would inquire of God to find the answer. In either situation, there was no contact with the living God because God dwelt in the Holy of Holies in unapproachable light, inaccessible to the common person.

Jesus had to break down Peter's old theology by showing him that the old way of finding the will of God by consulting the Law and the prophets had been eclipsed. The will and presence of God was no longer going to be discerned through a book or a consultation with a person. One can now go directly to God through a living relationship with Jesus Christ.

In John 13, Peter had another bombshell dropped on his theology. After three and a half years of following the Lord, he thought that, by this time, he had things figured out. Jesus was the Lord, and that made him the Lord's servant. But on the night of the Last Supper, in one of Christ's last gestures of love before going to the cross, Jesus knelt down like a common servant and began washing Peter's feet. Outraged and appalled (because Jesus had violated his theology—masters do not serve servants; servants serve masters), Peter vehemently rebuked the Lord, saying, "You shall never wash my feet, no, never, even to the ages of eternity!"

But Peter needed to be shown that unless he was willing to first let Jesus serve him, he could never be Jesus's disciple. Peter needed to have his theology rewritten again. First and foremost, Peter needed to learn to be a receiver. He needed to allow the Lord to wash the dust of this world off of his feet, refresh him, and fill him before he would ever be of any use in serving others.

Thoughts/Prayers

Of the shepherds mentioned in an earlier devotion, one of those whose life and work continues to influence countless Christians is A.B. Simpson. Born in 1843, Simpson was an eloquent preacher, theologian, author, hymn writer, and founder of the Christian and Missionary Alliance. Over the course of his lifetime, he wrote over a hundred books and a number of famous hymns. In midlife, he experienced divine healing from a chronic heart disorder, and although he believed in and preached on divine healing, he still maintained the proper perspective of lifting up the person of Christ rather than elevating his gifts. This is evidenced by the following verse from one of his famous hymns, "Once It Was the Blessing":

Once it was the blessing,
Now it is the Lord;
Once it was the feeling,
Now it is His Word;
Once His gift I wanted,
Now the Giver own;
Once I sought for healing,
Now Himself alone.

All in all forever,
Only Christ I'll sing;
Everything is in Christ,
And Christ is everything.

If you feel trapped behind a wall by an old way of doing things, if you are stuck in the religious rut of an old theology that is not bringing you any closer to the Lord, if you are suffocating within a stifling religious environment or suffering from some disappointment because the God you thought you knew has not met your expectations, it is time to lift your eyes to the one leaping upon the mountains and the hills. He is completely free. He wants you to join him where he is. He is the one who is calling to you: "Arise, my darling, my beautiful one, and come along!"

Initial Love

SONG OF SONGS, CHAPTER 2

"My beloved is mine, and I am his;
He pastures his flock among the lilies.
Until the cool of the day when the shadows flee away,
Turn, my beloved, and be like a gazelle
Or a young stag on the mountains of Bether."

SONG OF SONGS 2:16–17

The first phase in the maiden's understanding of her beloved's love is summarized in the verse, "My beloved is mine, and I am his" (Song of Songs 2:16) or by earlier verses in this section in which she says, "My beloved is to me..." (Song of Songs 1:13–14). This was a stage of discovery and revelation. Although she had come to know and love her king, the emphasis was primarily on herself—on what he was *to her*. She had not yet come to discover the wonder, the mystery, of what she was *to him*.

So far, she had seen and experienced:

- That the love of her beloved was better than anything this world had to offer (Song of Songs 1:2)
- That he was the king (Song of Songs 1:4)
- The contrast between who he is and who she was (Song of Songs 1:5)
- That she had been badly burned by trying to live under laws, rules, and outward activity that had distracted her (Song of Songs 1:6)
- That the shepherd-king had a flock and his own shepherds whom she could follow to find the rest and nourishment she was looking for (Song of Songs 1:8)

- That her beauty would come as a result of her beloved's gift, not from what she could produce on her own (Song of Songs 1:11)
- A greater revelation and appreciation for death and resurrection (Song of Songs 1:13–14)
- Rest and union with him and the knowledge that what was his was also hers (Song of Songs 1:16–17)
- Feasting at his banqueting table where his banner over her was love (Song of Songs 2:4)
- That her beloved was as free as a gazelle (Song of Songs 2:8–9)

Yet, although she had seen all these things and experienced them in part, they had not all been made a part of her life.

In this section, she also discovered that she was the rose of Sharon—something common and ordinary—but also that she was the king's lily (Song of Songs 2:1–2). In chapter 2, verse 16, she learned that "he pastures his flock among the lilies." The words "his flock" are inserted into the English text, so it should actually read, "he pastures (or feeds) among the lilies." What does this mean? There are two possible ways of viewing it: It may mean the king feeds his darling, his beautiful one, among other "lilies." Or it may mean the king himself feeds and finds contentment and satisfaction among the lilies. Either way, the point is that *there are others like her.* The lilies represent those with pure hearts who desperately seek after the Lord, as the maiden does.

In Matthew 6:28–30 Jesus said,

And why are you worried about clothing? Observe how the lilies of the field grow; they do not toil [work] nor do they spin [that is, spin wool], yet I say to you that not even Solomon in all his glory clothed himself like one of these. But if God so clothes the grass of the field, which is alive today and tomorrow is thrown into the furnace, will He not much more clothe you? You of little faith!

The lilies of the field do not work. They are at rest, clothed in the royal beauty with which God has endowed them. They stand tall, yet naturally bow over in a display of humility.

Paul, writing to Timothy in 1 Timothy 3:15, told his apprentice apostle how "one ought to conduct himself in the household of God, which is the church of the living God, the pillar and support of the truth." But writing again to him about five years later, when the church was in a state of decline, Paul likened the church to "a large house" in which "there are not only gold and silver vessels, but also vessels of wood and earthenware, and some to honor and some to dishonor. Therefore, if anyone cleanses himself from these things, he will be a vessel for honor, sanctified, useful to the Master, prepared for every good work" (2 Timothy 2:20–21).

As it was toward the end of the first century, in most parts of the world the church today is in a state of decline. Like at Ephesus (where Timothy was when he received Paul's letter), the church today has become a "large house." In a large house, there are the crowds—represented by those ordinary vessels of wood, which are common and more abundant. Today, the masses cram into church buildings and form a multitude, but most of them never really become known to one another or drawn into a deeper relationship with Christ.

In contrast to the vessels of wood, there are the vessels of gold and silver. They are costly and rare and have been through the fire of purification. We can learn from this contrast that God has a secret: he can be found among the few, not the many.

After he told Timothy to cleanse himself from "these things" (the vessels of wood and earthenware), Paul admonished him to "flee from youthful lusts and pursue righteousness, faith, love and peace *with those who call on the Lord from a pure heart*" (2 Timothy 2:22, emphasis mine).

Those who call on the Lord from a pure heart are the lilies. Among those lilies is where your Lord feeds and can be found!

Other examples of this principle can be seen in the Book of Exodus where we read that, originally, God intended for the whole nation of Israel to be a kingdom of priests (Exodus 19:3–6). But after Israel's unfaithfulness in worshiping the golden calf, the priesthood was allotted only to the tribe of Levi, who would then represent the whole nation.

In the Book of Ezra, King Cyrus sent out a written proclamation throughout his entire kingdom and put it in writing that whoever, among all the Jews, wanted to return from captivity in Babylon to Jerusalem to rebuild the temple of God could go and do so. He even guaranteed that their support would be provided. But only a remnant responded.

In the letters to the seven churches in the Book of Revelation, once again, we see the Spirit's call going out to all of God's people, but not all responding. Those who would respond, however, received the promise that they would be fed by the Lord himself and have intimate fellowship with him:

- To the church in Ephesus: "To him who overcomes, I will grant to eat of the tree of life which is in the Paradise of God." (Revelation 2:7)

- To the church at Pergamum: "To him who overcomes, to him I will give of the hidden manna." (Revelation 2:17)
- To the church in Laodicea: "Behold I stand at the door and knock, if anyone hears My voice and opens the door, I will come in to him and will dine with him, and he with Me." (Revelation 3:20)

This section of the Song closes with the maiden's cry: "Turn, my beloved, and be like a gazelle or a young stag on the mountains of Bether."

Bether means "separation." Mountains of separation had come between the maiden and her beloved. Although she knew that he fed among the lilies, she still felt estranged. Although she saw him as being free as a gazelle and able to leap upon the mountains, still she was holding back and had retreated behind a wall. Thankfully, love did not give up on her. Even in this condition, she was being drawn into a deeper stage of knowing and loving her beloved: the stage of increasing love.

PART 2: INCREASING LOVE

"I am my Beloved's and my Beloved is mine."

SONG OF SONGS 6:3

Where Can I Find My Beloved?

"Catch the foxes for us, the little foxes
That are ruining the vineyard,
While our vineyards are in blossom."

"My beloved is mine, and I am his;
He pastures his flock among the lilies.
Until the cool of the day when
The shadows flee away,
Turn my beloved, and be like a gazelle
Or a young stag on the mountains of Bether."

SONG OF SONGS 2:15–17

"On my bed night after night I sought him
Whom my soul loves;
I sought him but did not find him.
'I must arise now and go about the city;
In the streets and in the squares
I must seek him whom my soul loves.'
I sought him but did not find him.
The watchmen who make the rounds in the city found me,
And I said, 'Have you seen him whom my soul loves?'
Scarcely had I left them
When I found him whom my soul loves;
I held on to him and would not let him go
Until I had brought him to my mother's house,
And into the room of her who conceived me."

SONG OF SONGS 3:1–4

Hours later, I sat alone in my room pining and thinking. My beloved, I was sure, had gone away again. He had come to me and invited me to go with him to the country and to the high places, but I had been reluctant to go. The wall remained a barrier between us. Although he was prepared to take me away with him, I had not been ready.

Suddenly, I heard a knock on the door. When I opened it, one of the maidservants handed me a small scroll. "It is a message for you from the king," she said.

I was hesitant and even fearful as I broke the seal. There were only a few lines of writing on it. The note read:

> Catch the little foxes for us; the little foxes that are ruining the vineyards
> while our vineyards are in blossom.
>
> Solomon

"My beloved is mine, and I am his!" I whispered aloud with a sigh of relief. For reasons I could not fully understand, I knew that Solomon still loved me. Pausing for a moment, I reflected, *I know there are others in his kingdom—other lilies with whom he feeds and takes pleasure. I know that he must sometimes go away to be with them, for he is not only my king, but theirs as well. They need his protection and his attention, and they have hungry hearts to hear from him as well. But how I wish he would return to me! Hear my plea, Solomon. Turn, my beloved. Return to me. Be like a gazelle or a young stag on the mountains of Bether; the mountains that separate us!*

For days, I pondered the contents of the mysterious note. Was it a riddle? Night after night it kept me awake as I tossed and turned upon my bed. Then, late one night, a memory returned to me. It was of the day the king found me in my own neglected vineyard. I had been so distracted by my work then. But now, I realized, I had been distracted by all of my new comforts! I was living under the king's very roof. I had been waited on by his servants. I had been treated as though I were already his queen. I had tasted of luxury and bounty. But now, I understood that I had been once more distracted—only this time it was by all the good things he had given!

I picked up the short note and read the first part of it over again:

> Catch the little foxes for us; the little foxes that are ruining the vineyards.

My eyes were opened—as if by revelation. "Those vineyards represent my heart!" I said out loud in amazement. "The foxes have been nibbling away at what was intended to be entirely for him. I have been so inattentive to my own vineyard, once again, that I was not willing to go with him to see the vineyards that belong to *us*. He would not take me there against my will. Oh, Solomon! I must arise and look for my beloved!"

I quickly dressed and hurried out into the streets, searching the squares and thoroughfares. The watchmen patrolling the streets saw me. One of them approached me and inquired, "Do you need help, my dear?"

"Oh, yes, I do," I said. "Have you seen him whom my soul loves?"

The watchmen looked at one another knowingly as if they shared a secret. Peering down a narrow street off the main square, their eyes pointed in the direction that I should go.

I dashed down the street. Scarcely had I left the watchmen when I found him. He was sitting on a stone wall gazing up at the moon and the stars. I came upon him from behind, reached out to him, and clung to him, and oh, I would not let him go!

With both arms hugging his waist tightly as we walked together back to the residence, I said, "I realize that my heart has strayed from you, even while I was enjoying all the benefits of living under your roof. I am willing to leave it all behind if that is what you would require of me. Truly, my love, it all means nothing if you are not there. Where you are is where my home is, even if that should mean taking you back to my mother's house and to the small room in which she conceived me."

"You have learned a great lesson, my love," said the king. "The most valuable treasure we have in life is not found in things, but in each other."

I smiled. "I would take you there someday for other reasons as well," I said. "Your love to me is so wonderful, and you are so wise and so good. I would show you to those of my household so that they might rejoice with me!"

I was tired, and it was late. The king summoned the daughters of Jerusalem who cared for the residence. "Escort my love to her room," he said to them. "And I adjure you, O daughters, by the gazelles or the hinds of the field, that you will not arouse or awaken my love until she pleases."

I enjoyed a long, peaceful night's sleep that lasted late into the morning. Finally, I aroused myself and got dressed. One of my attendants had a message for me from the king. He wanted to meet for an early lunch.

I went with my attendants to the dining hall. The king was waiting there, and he greeted me with an eager smile. "You look beautiful as always, my dear. I hope you had a good night's rest."

"Your smile is unusually radiant this morning, my king," I said as he greeted me with a short kiss. "Are you going to tell me what provokes in you such happiness?"

"I will—on a full stomach," he responded with a grin.

We sat down at the table that had been prepared for us. The servants inquired what we wanted to eat and then filled our plates with an assortment of meats, breads, nuts, and dried fruits.

After several bites, the king put down his fork and began, "The time has come for us to prepare for our wedding day, my darling."

My heart leapt to my throat.

"You appear as if you are in shock, my love," said the king, laughing slightly.

"Never have I been so at a loss for words!" I was finally able to utter. "I have dreamed of hearing those words roll from your lips since the day we first met! From your actions I have known what you intended—but to hear the words still causes my heart to leap. You are indeed wonderful—the fulfiller of all my dreams! I could not be happier! How do you envision the wedding to be? How shall we begin to prepare?"

His dark eyes shone with love, but I saw something else in them too—something that caused me to pause. "I too have waited and longed for that day when we finally will become man and wife," he said. "For me, my love, it could not come too soon. But first, it is necessary for something else to occur. In a few days you must leave this place and go away for a time."

The joy quickly drained from my face.

"But… what do you mean?" I asked. "Such a mixture of news—both sweet and bitter. Please explain, for I am confused. What reason is there that we should be apart?"

Seeing my hurt, he rushed to reassure me. "Let me assure you, there is nothing I want more than to be together with you—*forever!*" he replied. "But you must not forget that you will not be marrying just a common man. You will be marrying a king! The God of heaven has granted me charge over a kingdom. Portions of this kingdom you have seen, but there are other portions you have not seen. I want you to know my whole realm, and part of that realm is the wilderness. Although you will walk throughout this whole land, you must never forget that part of my kingdom is barren and without fruit, yet it is still under my rule. I want you to learn to live, walk, and abide there as well. As harsh as my instruction may seem, you will come to understand: the wilderness is a place where you will learn things you can learn nowhere else, things that will prepare you for our life together. What you discover there will only make our love stronger." He searched my face and smiled as I nodded.

He continued, "Although I will not be going with you, I will send someone to accompany you—my mother, Queen Bathsheba. She was the beloved wife of my father David. She has wanted to spend time with you ever since she learned that I had fallen in love and wanted you to be my wife. I want you to get to know her. Her father, Ahithopel, was King David's counselor. My mother is a very wise woman. She knows what it is like to be a queen, and she knows my ways. I lean greatly on her advice. You will learn much from her."

"I trust that what you say is true and needful, my king, but it gives me only slight comfort," I said. Even so, I forced myself to be brave. I could hear the understanding in his voice, yet I found it hard to believe his words.

"Believe me, I understand what you are feeling, but it will be for the best," he said. "While you are there, I will send the kingdom's finest tailor to work on your wedding dress and a company of my mighty men to protect you. You will not see my soldiers, but they will be very close by. When you are ready to leave the wilderness, they will escort you back to me upon my royal couch, carrying you on their shoulders.

"Meanwhile, I have a place to prepare for you! When you see me again, it will be on our wedding day. I will be riding to meet you upon a traveling throne that I will fashion with my own hands from the timbers of Lebanon. We will share it, my darling. Its back will be made of gold, its seat of purple cloth, and its interior of exquisite embroidered fabric, and it will be carried along by my servants on posts of silver. Following our day of gladness, I will take your hand, and you will mount my throne with me. Then we will ride off together as man and wife!"

POINTS TO CONSIDER

Song of Songs 3:1 reads, "On my bed night after night I sought him." Notice the change in wording, indicative of longing and loss: what was once "our" couch is now "my" bed. The maiden had become so comfortable in her circumstances that she didn't realize her bridegroom had departed! We see her now on her bed, night after night, still behind the wall of separation. Distraught over the perceived loss of her beloved's presence, she can no longer stay in her place of comfort apart from being with him.

"Mountains of Bether" literally means "mountains of separation."

When the desire to change her circumstances finally became stronger than her tolerance for the pain she was experiencing on her comfortable bed, she left behind the familiar and responded to the king's call to "Arise!" And immediately after contacting the watchmen, she found the one whom her soul loved.

Our journey to spiritual maturity is intensely personal, but we cannot reach it on our own. Like the maiden, we sometimes need to seek help from others in the body of Christ (the watchmen) who are waiting and watching for him as well.

The Lord can speak to us directly, but he also speaks to us through other believers, and that, sometimes, is how we find him and pick up the trail in our pursuit of him.

This was a basic lesson that even the apostles needed to learn. Following the resurrection, it was Mary Magdalene to whom the Lord first appeared. She was a woman, not one of the mighty apostles. When she ran back from the tomb to the place where they were gathered and reported that Jesus had risen and that she had seen him alive, they didn't believe her. Nor did they believe the report from the two who saw him on the road to Emmaus. Even the apostles acted like atheists when it came to believing that the Lord could speak through anyone but themselves!

> Now after He had risen early on the first day of the week, He first appeared to Mary Magdalene, from whom He had cast out seven demons. She went and reported to those who had been with Him, while they were mourning and weeping. When they heard that He was alive and had been seen by her, they refused to believe it. After that, He appeared in a different form to two of them while they were walking along on their way to the country. They went away and reported it to the others, but they did not believe them either. (Mark 16:9–13)

The apostles needed to learn the lesson that they were not the heads of the church—Jesus was, and Jesus is. He can speak with authority through any member of his body he chooses to use. He is not restricted to speaking only from the "top down" through those purported to be in leadership.

Jesus Christ, the invisible, unseen head of the church, wants to become visible and to express himself on this earth. He does this through his body. No one individual is capable of expressing the fullness of Christ, any more than a person's little finger alone can portray what his whole body looks like.

Finding him after her contact with the watchmen, the maiden clung to him and wanted to bring him "into my mother's house, and into the room of her who conceived me." Here, "my mother's house" represents the church. Paul, writing to the Galatian churches, told them that "the Jerusalem above is free; she is our mother" (Galatians 4:27). Like Mary and those on the road to Emmaus, when people see the Lord, what do they want to do? They want to rush back to the church and share their revelation of him with others!

Oh Lord, when you appear to me after a long absence, I want to cling to you and never let you go. But you are the Lord. You are the king. You are the head of your church. You can come and go freely as you please. I cannot hold you or make you stay by my own grip or through my own efforts.

Show yourself not only to me, but to others in your body. Open my heart to receive what you have to say through all of those you send my way.

Lord, I want to show you off and let others see you, because you are beautiful beyond compare. Let me take you to my mother's house. Give me opportunities to share what I've known of you with others in your body.

Plant me among other lilies and reveal yourself so that you can be honored, seen, and glorified.

"For they say among the Jews, care is taken that no one who has not attained full maturity be allowed so much as to hold the [Song of Songs] in his hands…

"We must come to this sacred marriage of the Bridegroom and the Bride with the understanding proper to interior love—come, that is, dressed in a wedding garment lest, if we are not attired in a wedding garment, we be cast out of the wedding feast into the outer darkness, the blindness of ignorance."

Origen of Alexandria, third century

From the Wilderness to the Wedding

SONG OF SONGS, CHAPTER 3

"Who is this coming up from the wilderness
Like columns of smoke,
Perfumed with myrrh and frankincense,
With all scented powders of the merchant?
Behold, the traveling couch of Solomon;
Sixty mighty men around it,
Of the mighty men of Israel.
All of them are wielders of the sword,
Expert in war;
Each man has his sword at his side,
Guarding against the terrors of the night.
King Solomon has made for himself a sedan chair
From the timber of Lebanon.
He made its posts of silver,
Its back of gold
And its seat of purple fabric,
With its interior lovingly fitted out
By the daughters of Jerusalem."
"Go forth, O daughters of Zion,
And gaze on King Solomon with the crown
With which his mother has crowned him
On the day of his wedding,
And on the day of his gladness of heart."

SONG OF SONGS 3:6—11

Nearly the whole city of Jerusalem turned out to line the streets and welcome the wedding procession. Young and old alike anxiously watched to catch a glimpse of me and participate in this festive occasion. As I neared the city, I could hear the buzz among the onlookers as the crowds mounted, inquiring of one another, "Who is this coming up out of the wilderness to be wed with the king?"

In some ways, I wondered the same question myself. Who was I, now? Solomon's love had changed me. The wilderness, too, had forever altered my soul. What I had seen and experienced there would forever be held close to my heart—my secret pain, the grief of not being with him, and yet, the revelation—it was all too deep for words. I smiled. The wilderness had not been a pleasant place—but having been there only heightened my thirst to know more of his love.

I observed with wonder as people scrambled to get into the best positions to witness this historic event. Soldiers tried to keep the crowds orderly so that the canopied litter in which I was riding could pass by. I heard the frustrated cries of those standing toward the back, away from the street, yelling, "I can't see! I can't see!"

My couch was carried by sixty of the king's mighty warriors, bedecked with their magnificent swords. Musicians paraded before and behind, playing on their lyres, pipes, horns, cymbals, and tambourines. Pillars of smoke wafted upward from the censers carried by scores of incense-bearers, the smoke announcing my arrival far into the distance. The air was thick with the smell of myrrh and frankincense. As I entered the city, loud choruses from those on the streets and standing on the rooftops greeted me as they thrust their arms in the air, jubilantly exclaiming, "Behold, the traveling couch of Solomon!"

I tried to imagine King Solomon leaving his royal residence and entering the courtyard where his own portable throne awaited. He would step up into the compartment dressed in stately robes perfumed with myrrh, aloes, and cassia. He would be wearing the flowered crown his mother had made for him, not his usual circlet of gold to display his authority, but a crown of joy made especially for his wedding day.

The activity in the streets faded before my mind's eye. My heart was in the courtyard, mounting a throne, coming to greet me. A team of strong soldiers would grasp the long, silver supporting rods and slowly, uniformly, hoist his palanquin to their shoulders. At the command of the captain, they would begin to march in a slow cadence to meet up with the bridal procession.

It was not only imagination, I knew. Even now, he would be coming to me.

Joy pounded inside my breast. I thought to myself that the God of heaven must be looking down with delight to see our separate processions approaching one another, preparing to merge into one, much as he delighted when the first man and woman wove their way through Eden's garden in anticipation of seeing each other for the first time. Surely, God rejoiced to see our desire to become one, as he rejoiced to see the first couple unleash their passions to become one flesh.

The two processions met and came to a stop at the steps of the royal palace. My heart raced as I looked past the thousands of eyes that were riveted upon the two compartments in which King Solomon and I were hidden from view. As his throne appeared in my sight, my solitary obsession was to have my first glimpse of him.

He was the first to step down from his compartment. The crowds burst into deafening shouts of joy and applauded wildly. As the noise subsided, I stepped down from my couch. A second thunderous ovation erupted.

The folds of my magnificent wedding gown moved around me. It was interwoven with gold and made of exquisite embroidered work. Accompanying me were my mother, brothers, relatives, and friends, along with other young maidens and daughters of Jerusalem. Their laughter and shouts of joy expressed all I felt within as I moved toward my king, riding a rising swell of gladness.

When I finally met the king and stood before him, I was breathless. He looked just as I had imagined. I bowed low before him in reverence, desiring to communicate to him even a token of the honor which he alone deserved. Then I looked up and saw his face. It was aglow. He was enraptured by my appearance. I blushed deeply and smiled behind my translucent veil. Our eyes met for but a moment, and immediately we embraced, holding on to one another with all of our strength. Then we turned and mounted the steps, arm in arm, to enter the palace hall and the great throne room.

Inside the palace, a majestic choir of Levitical priests, consisting of four thousand singers and musicians, awaited us around the circumference of the room. The aging Zadok, faithful high priest during David's reign and now that of Solomon, presided over the ceremony. He welcomed all the guests.

Zadok was dressed in his dark blue, priestly robe, which was laced with golden threads and hung to his knees. The skirt of his garment was lined with embroidered pomegranate blossoms of blue, purple, and scarlet, and between them, golden bells. Covering his chest was the breastplate bearing twelve jewels, each engraved with the name of one of the twelve tribes of Israel. Upon his head was a turban made of a long band of white linen. And on the front of the turban, on his forehead, was a golden plate upon which were inscribed the words, "Holiness to Jehovah." Solomon and I stood before him. His eyes sparkled as he looked upon us as a father would a beloved son and daughter.

Following his opening remarks, Zadok slowly raised his right hand in the air and gazed around the room at the choir of priests, appearing to examine each one of them. Their eyes were all fixed upon him, awaiting his command. Then, as he clutched his hand into a fist and forcefully swung his arm in a downward motion, the choir burst forth in song.

It was like thunder. Never could one have gauged the power or anticipated the splendor of those voices. The choruses they sang were filled with the highest, most sublime range of crescendos, only to be followed by decrescendos, making their soft and pleasant landing in sweet harmonies that soothed the soul like nothing I had ever before experienced. It seemed as if the choir of heaven itself had been granted divine leave of its realm for a brief while, and we mortals were allowed to hear the sound of angels' voices, singing as they sing around the throne of God.

When the choir was finished, they sat down. Left standing were only the sons of Korah, whom Solomon had commissioned to compose a special song of love to celebrate our marriage. Their hearts seemed to overflow as they addressed their verses to the king, singing of the grace that had been poured upon his lips; of his throne, which had been established forever; and of God's anointing him with the oil of joy above his fellows. Of me they sang too: that I was all glorious within and without, describing even my wedding gown. Those words will live in my memory forever as an inspired psalm. A song for the ages.

When they concluded, the king's mother read to us a blessing which she had composed for this special occasion. It was comprised of two parts, the first dedicated to Solomon and the second to me. To Solomon she began, "Oh, son of mine, do not waste your life chasing after many women. This has ruined many kings." Turning to me, she recited a beautiful exhortation which began, "An excellent wife, who can find? For her worth is far above jewels. The heart of her husband trusts in her, and she will have no lack of gain. She does him good and not evil all the days of her life."

By the time Queen Bathsheba had finished, my eyes were swimming with tears of joy. I took one fleeting glance at the assembly of guests in the large hall who had been invited for this solemn but joyous event. In particular, I noted the daughters of Zion. Their faces were aglow. Like mirrors, they seemed to reflect the radiance they beheld on the face of King Solomon. I imagined that each one of them must have been stirred by a deep longing from within—that one day soon each would meet her own king.

Points to Consider

The proper translation for verse 6, chapter 3, is "Who is this coming up from the wilderness," not "What is this" as is found in many translations. Moreover, the wording is feminine. It was the bride coming up out of the wilderness. Solomon had sent for her with his emissary of mighty men who were to protect her on her way to meet him.

Life with our heavenly king is not always a beautiful fairy tale. Often, we encounter great difficulties which reach far beyond any plans or expectations we have about the journey of life. We all must face our own wilderness experiences.

The wilderness is a dry place. It tests the very fibers of our being. It reduces to ashes the shallow motives of the heart. It purges us of unrealistic love. It burns away the dross of a love meant to withstand all things. But the wilderness is also the place where we develop intense thirst for God. "O God, You are my God; I shall seek you earnestly; My soul thirsts for You, my flesh longs for You, in a dry and weary land where there is no water" (Psalm 63:1).

The maiden now pictures for us one who has passed through the fiery trials of suffering and emerges from the wilderness giving off new fragrances, having been transformed by the spiritual experiences and lessons she learned there. The refiner's fire has burned away her dross and left in its place pillars of smoke. She has become, as Paul wrote, a "fragrance of Christ to God among those who are being saved and among those who are perishing; to the one an aroma from death to death, to the other an aroma from life to life. And who is adequate for these things?" (2 Corinthians 2:15).

These new graces do not come without cost. Song of Songs 3:6 says that she was perfumed "with all scented powders of the merchant." The merchant mentioned in the verse is the Lord Jesus. She has paid him through the sufferings she endured to acquire the sweet-smelling aromas that are now manifest in her life through the purifying work of the Holy Spirit.

"Behold, it is the traveling couch of Solomon" in verse 7 could also read, "Behold, the couch of Solomon!"

In other translations "couch" is translated as *bed, litter,* or *sedan chair.* The word is best translated *palanquin,* which means a wheelless vehicle or human-powered transport. Such transports have been known as *sedan chairs* in England, *palanquins* in India, and *gamas* in Korea. In the early twentieth century these palanquins, or traveling couches, which were supported on either side by two long poles that rested on the shoulders of men, all but disappeared and were replaced by wheeled rickshaws, which were much more practical.

Solomon's royal palanquin was made of wood, gold, silver, and purple fabric. The wood and the gold are reminders of the furniture in the tabernacle, which were made of wood overlaid with gold. God comes to us in the perfect blend of divinity (gold) and humanity (wood), which is the essence of the God-man, our bridegroom, the Lord Jesus.

The posts, the supporting rods of Solomon's palanquin, were made of silver. Silver in the Scripture represents redemption. This signifies that the Lord comes to us upon the strength of his redeeming love. Purple represents royalty, and the purple fabric upon which Solomon was seated represents the kingliness and authority of Jesus, the King of all kings.

Psalm 45 is a wedding song. For certain, it is a Messianic Psalm, speaking of Christ and his bride, the church. The exact king of whom it was written at the time is uncertain. However, the consensus of most scholars is that it was Solomon. (The question is unsettled because certain warlike descriptions of him do not seem to apply.)

Most scholars credit Bathsheba with writing Proverbs 31. It begins with, "The words of King Lemuel, the oracle which his mother taught him." Solomon is referred to here as *Lemuel,* or the one "belonging to God." Portions of this proverb could have been read or written for the king and his bride on their wedding day.

In the final scene in this passage, there is an admonition by a mysterious third party (representing the Holy Spirit) to the daughters of Zion: "Go forth and gaze upon King Solomon with his crown." The Spirit wants us to see what joy it brings the king to be involved in this love relationship with the maiden. Behold his gladness of heart. See how happy he is when he finds one who responds to his love and who loves him in return!

THOUGHTS/PRAYERS

Oh, Lord Jesus, I long to see your face. I long for the day that I will stand before you and become joined eternally with you to be your lover, your friend, your companion, and your life partner for the ages. Lord, thank you that the momentary, light afflictions that I am experiencing in my wildernesses are producing for me an eternal weight of glory far beyond all comparison. Thank you, dear Refiner, for plunging me into the trials of fire that I was destined for in this life so that you can burn away all dross and produce in me a pleasing fragrance to you. Thank you, dear Deliverer, for sustaining me and protecting me each step of my journey. Thank you, sovereign and mighty King, for your plan and for the lavish celebration you have prepared for me and for all the redeemed. Thank you, Beloved and Radiant One, that although I might not always see or believe it, I do make your heart glad.

Ravishing!

SONG OF SONGS, CHAPTER 4

"How beautiful you are, my darling,
How beautiful you are!
Your eyes are like doves behind your veil;
Your hair is like a flock of goats
That have descended from Mount Gilead.
Your teeth are like a flock of newly shorn ewes
Which have come up from their washing,
All of which bear twins,
And not one among them has lost her young.
Your lips are like a scarlet thread,
And your mouth is lovely
Your temples are like a slice of a pomegranate
Behind your veil.
Your neck is like the tower of David,
Built with rows of stones
On which are hung a thousand shields,
All the round shields of the mighty men.
Your two breasts are like two fawns,
Twins of a gazelle
Which feed among the lilies.
Until the cool of the day
When the shadows flee away,
I will go my way to the mountain of myrrh

And to the hill of frankincense.
You are altogether beautiful, my darling,
And there is no blemish in you."

SONG OF SONGS 4:1–7

The time had come for us to be joined as man and wife. Solomon drew close to me, reached out, and took my two hands in his. Then he spoke from his heart, with words intended for my ears alone. Here is what he said:

"My darling, this is the happiest moment of my life. You are beautiful beyond compare. You are ravishing—no, breathtaking to behold. To describe what I see when I look at you, I must draw upon everything in Israel that I prize for beauty." He smiled tenderly and drew me into his arms.

"Your beauty is not only physical. There is also a beauty about you that is unseen. That hidden woman of the heart is just as beautiful as the lovely creature I now hold in my arms.

"Your stunning, dark eyes captivate me. They are like the eyes of a dove that can see but one thing at a time, and I know that they see only me. Yet, they are hidden from the world behind your veil. The look of love that you have for me is something only the two of us can comprehend. Know that I will always treasure that love.

"Your thick, wavy hair flows gracefully down upon your shoulders, like the beauty of a flock of goats winding their way down from Mount Gilead. It is a symbol to me of your submissive heart. For, from your heart, not only do you comply with my every wish, but you willingly serve this kingdom and the King above all kings, whom I serve as well. And as the name *Mount Gilead* means 'the hill of testimony,' so has your submissive heart become a testimony to all who have come to know you.

"Your rows of lovely white teeth remind me of a flock of newly shorn ewes which have come up from their washing. They all bear twins. But they too are a sign of something deeper that I value in you. When babies are young, they are only able to drink milk. But when they grow teeth, they are able to chew and take in solid food. So it is with you, my love. Unlike the simple and immature, you have the spiritual capacity to assimilate wisdom and take in the deeper things of God. In you, I have found one with whom I can share my very heart.

"Your lips are a deep and beautiful red, like a scarlet thread. Their crimson color is a symbol to me of the blood of the redeeming lambs sacrificed at the temple. For when you speak, you speak with redeeming words. As my mother so aptly expressed when she read her blessing to you, 'You open your mouth in wisdom, and the teaching of kindness is on your tongue.' Your mouth is lovely. Your smile is one of infectious charm; a smile of joy!

"Your temples, my darling, are like a slice of pomegranate. The rows of juicy, red seeds from the pomegranate speak of the abundant life within that fruit. When opened, it is a fruit of beauty, of passion and of richness. Of all the fruits served, it will always elicit the greatest sighs of pleasure and appreciation. Like the pomegranate, you are so full of life, my love! But that life is also partially concealed behind your veil, speaking to me of the dignity you possess. You are not one to flaunt yourself, nor to make a show of who you are.

"Your neck is strong like the citadel of David which towers above the city of Jerusalem, protecting it from attack. You have a strong will, my love, but it is as David's tower, strong in protecting the things of God. And around your neck is the necklace I sent with my mother for you as a wedding gift, to give to you on this special day. It is laced with row upon row of tiny shields numbering one thousand. These are but symbols of the protection that will surround you every day of your life. And so it will be as long as you shall live. But they are also symbols of the faith you possess in the living God, which will withstand any fiery darts that should be hurled against you.

"Your two breasts are youthful, like two fawns, the twins of a gazelle, which feed among the lilies. Although you are innocent, you have reached maturity. As my queen, you will be called upon to counsel and to nourish others, and so has God endowed you.

"The sweet aroma of your presence is to me more than the mere scent of myrrh, more than a whiff of the beauty of frankincense—you are as a mountain of myrrh; a hill of the most intoxicating incense! I am intoxicated by your presence. I am ready to spend my life going to that mountain and to that hill to find my delight. You are altogether beautiful, my darling, and there is no blemish in you!"

When the king had finished with these words, we turned to face Zadok, and we were married in the sight of God and man.

POINTS TO CONSIDER

Doves have no peripheral vision. They can only focus on one thing at a time. They also mate only once, and that for life—such a beautiful description from nature of the single-mindedness of the bride for her king!

Hair, in the Scriptures, represents submission to authority, obedience, and consecration. Nazirites were those who vowed to abstain from wine, grapes, and any intoxicating drink (Numbers 6:1–21). They were forbidden to cut their hair or touch any dead thing. This was a vow one took to be separated completely for service to God.

Mount Gilead, which means "hill of testimony," is located in Jordan, and from there one can view the Promised Land. The bride's hair being compared to a flock of goats descending from Mount Gilead indicates that she had established a testimony. As Peter wrote concerning wives, her behavior was chaste and respectful, and her adornment was not merely external, but was "the hidden person of the heart, with the imperishable quality of a gentle and quiet spirit, which is precious in the sight of God" (1 Peter 3:1–4).

Her teeth speak of her spiritual capacity to take in solid food, and not only drink milk, which is for spiritual babes.

> And I, brethren, could not speak to you as to spiritual men, but as to men of flesh, as to infants in Christ. I gave you milk to drink, not solid food; for you were not yet able to receive it. (1 Corinthians 3:1–2)

The shields speak of her faith, as we can see in Paul's admonition in Ephesians: "Take up the full armor of God so that you will be able to stand firm against the schemes of the devil," including "the shield of faith with which you will be able to extinguish all the flaming arrows of the evil one" (Ephesians 6:13 and 16).

Finally, he says, "You are altogether beautiful, my darling, and there is no blemish in you" (Song of Songs 4:7). This reminds us of what Paul wrote to the Ephesians concerning the mystery of the husband and wife relationship, which is a picture of Christ and the church: "that He might present to Himself the church in all her glory, having no spot or wrinkle or any such thing; but that she would be holy and blameless" (Ephesians 5:27).

From before the foundation of the world, God the Father chose us and gave us as a gift to his beloved Son (John 17:6; Ephesians 1:3–4). No one can snatch us out of the Father's hand, or out of Christ's hand, for Christ and the Father are one (John 10:27–28). We were saved *by* Christ and are being kept *for* Christ (Jude 1:1). One day we will be presented *to* Christ.

> Now to Him who is able to keep you from stumbling, and to make you stand in the presence of His glory blameless with great joy, to the only God and Savior, through Jesus Christ our Lord, be glory, majesty, dominion and authority, before all time and now and forever. Amen. (Jude 1:25)

To be presented to the King and to stand before his glory blameless and with great joy—what a day that will be! And what a day it will be for the King as well— the day of his "gladness of heart" (Song of Songs 3:11)!

Lord Jesus, am I far enough along in my transformation process that you can see in me the qualities Solomon saw in this maiden? I know that I am a work in progress but that you always see more in me than I see in myself. You say in your Word that as a person "thinks in his heart, so is he" (Proverbs 23:7, NKJV). Give me grace to see and accept your assessment of me as all that matters and all that is true. I am your trophy. I am your workmanship.

Thank you, Lord, that you are faithful. Thank you that you will finish the work you have begun in me, as your Word says; and that you see the end from the beginning. Thank you that I will one day stand in your holy presence, blameless and with great joy.

I give myself to you. Finish your work in me as you did in the life of the Shulammite.

To the Mountains!

SONG OF SONGS, CHAPTER 4

"Come with me from Lebanon, my bride,
May you come with me from Lebanon
Journey down from the summit of Amana,
From the summit of Senir and Hermon,
From the dens of lions,
From the mountains of leopards.
You have made my heart beat faster, my sister, my bride;
You have made my heart beat faster with a single glance of your eyes,
With a single strand of your necklace.
How beautiful is your love, my sister, my bride!
How much better is your love than wine,
And the fragrance of your oils
Than all kinds of spices!
Your lips, my bride, drip honey;
Honey and milk are under your tongue,
And the fragrance of your garments is like the fragrance of Lebanon."

SONG OF SONGS 4:8–11

The wedding ceremony ended, and it was time for us to depart. I whispered in my bride's ear, "Come, my love! It is now time for us to celebrate our marriage. We will leave Jerusalem and go to the mountains of Lebanon. It is my favorite place in the entire kingdom. The views from there are breathtaking and heavenly. You will see things from Lebanon's lofty heights that you will never forget. I want to show you the far reaches of my kingdom and my inheritance, which we will share together all the rest of our days. What is mine is now yours. I want you to see it all."

Taking my hand, she entered with me through the curtains into the cozy compartment of my palanquin. It was exquisite within—a place of utter privacy, with a large couch upon which to recline. We felt ourselves gently rise as my mighty men lifted the coach into the air, causing it to rest upon their shoulders.

Inside, now husband and wife, we snuggled close to one another. She rested her head upon my shoulder.

Then, pulling back and looking me straight in the eye with excitement in her own, she said, "Tell me more about this place you are taking me—these mountains of Lebanon!"

I said, "It is a place which words cannot adequately describe. You must see it for yourself. From those towering heights alone you will be able to see our entire domain—the rivers, the valleys, the forests, the plains, the cities, the villages—all that is ours. But to get there and return again, danger and adventure await us. There will be treacherous paths and wild animals. We will pass the dens of lions and leopards. There remain some things within this kingdom that have not yet been tamed. But do not be afraid. There will not be a single moment when you are not protected."

"From the day that you first stole me away in your chariot and brought me to the palace, life has been but one great adventure," she said, her face beaming. She snuggled closer to me and rested her chin against my arm, looking up in my eyes. "Wherever we go, I will not be afraid, just as long as you are there."

At last, we were alone as husband and wife. The moment would soon come when the passion I had held in check for months would no longer need be restrained.

My eyes moved from her eyes down to her neck and then to her chest. There, draped over her breasts, was the wedding gift I had commissioned to be made for her—the necklace composed of a thousand shields. Grasping one of the shields between my fingers, I said to her, "Do you remember the shields that you saw hanging in my banqueting hall? I gave you this necklace to remind you that there will be a thousand times in the course of our union when you will be asked to trust me. If you ever become afraid, grasp one of these small shields and have faith in me. I will never be far from you, and I will always protect you."

We did not get far outside of Jerusalem that day. We were accompanied by a host of servants, cooks, soldiers, and an array of others. When we got to the Jordan River, we turned north and proceeded on our way to the hill country. Shortly, we found a lovely shaded area in which to set up camp for the night.

The soldiers lowered the couch to the ground in a grassy area only a short distance from the bank of the river. Soon there were fires, music, and from the trained hands of the best of chefs, a sumptuous meal brought to us inside our private compartment. We had a lovely view from a window which faced Jordan's gently flowing waters. We ate at our leisure, sipped wine, and talked. The soldiers spread out in a semicircle, forming a perimeter at a distance from our private shelter. We would not emerge from our seclusion that evening, but spend the entire night immersed in one another's love.

As nightfall descended, we took one final glance outside at the starry sky and the silvery moonbeams that spread across the river.

"How beautiful is your love, my sister, my bride!" I said. "How much better is your love than wine, and the fragrance of your oils than the mixtures of earth's grandest spices! Your lips drip with honey. Honey and milk are under your tongue. The fragrance of your garments is like heaven itself—like the fragrance of Lebanon."

With that, our lips met.

I gently slid my left hand under her head and my right hand around her waist. Soon, we were lost in one another's embraces and caresses. The moment we had both waited for so very long had come at last. We consummated our union that blissful evening and then drifted off peacefully to sleep in one another's arms.

POINTS TO CONSIDER

This was the first time in the Song of Songs that the king called the maiden his "bride." They were now united as husband and wife.

When Jesus Christ was raised from the dead, he was seated at God's right hand in heavenly realms, "far above all rule and authority and power and dominion, and every name that is named, not only in this age, but also in the one to come" (Ephesians 1:20–21). But the Scriptures teach that we were also made alive and seated in heavenly places with him.

Even when we were dead in our transgressions, [God] made us alive together with Christ (by grace you have been saved), and raised us up with Him, and seated us with Him in the heavenly places in Christ Jesus. (Ephesians 2:5–6)

Blessed be the God and Father of our Lord Jesus Christ, who has blessed us with every spiritual blessing in the heavenly places in Christ. (Ephesians 1:3)

The first thing King Solomon wanted to do once he married his bride was to take her to the mountains of Lebanon and give her a heavenly view of his kingdom and all that they shared. In the same way, Jesus Christ brought us with him and seated us with him in heavenly places at his resurrection. Now he wants to show us all that is ours "in him."

Although the Scriptures clearly teach that we are seated with Christ in heavenly places, still, we have a need. What is that need? We need to *see it!* We need our eyes opened. We need to look down from our lofty perch and see all that is ours because of our union with Christ—and then to come down from that mountain view and walk in it!

The secret is that this vast inheritance which we enjoy—an inheritance which is Christ himself—can only become real to us by revelation.

It takes God to reveal God. Unless God reveals himself to us, though we may be fabulously rich, we will walk as though we were paupers!

Coming down from the mountains, the king's bride passed through the dens of lions and the mountains of leopards, which represent the prowling, roaring, wicked forces of evil. To be one with him in all things means there will be times of spiritual warfare. In the highest heavens—"far above all rule and authority and everything that has a name"—we have been seated with Christ. But there are unseen realms in heavenly places where the spiritual powers of darkness still rule and make war with God's people. Paul wrote,

> Put on the full armor of God, so that you will be able to stand firm against the schemes of the devil. For our struggle [our battle, our jihad, our wrestling] is not against flesh and blood, but against the rulers, against the powers, against the world forces of this darkness, against the spiritual forces of wickedness in the heavenly places. (Ephesians 6:11–12)

> For though we walk in the flesh, we do not war according to the flesh, for the weapons of our warfare are not of the flesh, but divinely powerful for the destruction of fortresses, destroying speculations and every lofty thing raised up against the knowledge of God, and taking every thought captive to the obedience of Christ. (2 Corinthians 10:3–5)

Although Christ has conquered, although he reigns as King of kings and Lord of lords, and although all enemies are beneath his feet, yet he has called us to be part of this battle. We must stand against these enemies and wrestle them to the ground, pinning them down through the empowerment of his mighty, forceful strength which is at work within us.

Not all our enemies are external. Some are also internal—thoughts, speculations, false concepts—anything that keeps us from a true knowledge of Christ. In addition, there is the insidious enemy of pride.

Paul was caught up to the third heaven. He "heard inexpressible words, which a man is not permitted to speak" (2 Corinthians 12:4). But he tells us that, because of the surpassing greatness of the revelations, a thorn was given to him—a satanic messenger—to keep him from exalting himself. With great revelation comes the temptation to succumb to pride, which is always ready to spring up from within and rob God of his glory.

In the Song of Songs, Solomon was moved by just a single glance of his loved one's eyes and a single strand of her necklace—his gift to her. The thousand tiny shields represent the faith we have been given to stand against our enemies. Just a single shield—just a little faith—coupled with a look into the King's eyes, is all it takes for him to deliver us from danger.

Thoughts/Prayers

Lord, take me to the mountains. I have asked you to kiss me and to show me the affections of your love. I have asked you to draw me so that I will run after you. Now I ask you, Father, to open my eyes so that I can view from the mountaintop all of the riches of my inheritance in Christ.

Show me that I am seated with you and in you. Let me see you as my Defender, who wrestles and fights on my behalf against my enemies. Only you can reveal yourself to me. I ask you to do that, because I know that it excites your heart. I ask this in Jesus's name. Amen.

The Romantic Gardener

SONG OF SONGS, CHAPTER 4

"A garden locked is my sister, my bride;
A rock garden locked, a spring sealed up.
Your shoots are an orchard of pomegranates
With choice fruits, henna with nard plants,
Nard and saffron, calamus and cinnamon,
With all the trees of frankincense,
Myrrh and aloes, along with all the finest spices.
You are a garden spring,
A well of fresh water,
And streams flowing from Lebanon."

"Awake, O north wind,
And come, wind of the south;
Make my garden breathe out fragrance,
Let its spices be wafted abroad
May my beloved come into his garden
And eat its choice fruits!"

"I have come into my garden, my sister, my bride;
I have gathered my myrrh along with my balsam
I have eaten my honeycomb and my honey;
I have drunk my wine and my milk."

"Eat, friends;
Drink and imbibe deeply, O lovers."

SONG OF SONGS 4:12—16, 5:1

A month or so after we had returned to Jerusalem from Lebanon, I planned a special outing for my new bride and myself.

"Do you remember the first time I took you away in my chariot to visit the royal palace?" I asked her one morning.

"How could I forget, my king?" she replied. "It was a day that changed my life forever!"

"By now, you have come to know my love for God's creation—the wondrous variety of herbs, plants, flowers, and trees that are here for us to enjoy. One thing you saw that day in your brief tour of my residence was the garden. It is a place where I often retreat to find peace and solitude. There I have come to understand, in part, the wisdom of God in putting the first couple in charge of keeping Eden's garden, for this vocation does not only provide much enjoyment, but also many new discoveries. Today, my love, I would like to take you to my private garden."

"Oh yes! Let us go together," she said. "I will have the servants prepare a basket with some things to eat and a flask of water for us to take along."

Within the hour, we left the palace and strolled down a path until we came to a high stone wall. We approached the iron gate which was secured with a large lock. Removing a key from my pocket, I opened the gate. Then I took her by the hand, and we went inside.

It was a beautiful, sunny summer day. The skies were blue, and the temperatures were not too hot. We strolled down the center of the groomed pebble path with its stone borders. On either side of the path was a floral paradise. From the dark, rich soil grew varieties of bushes, plants, and trees of all sizes, all meticulously cared for. Between them were areas set apart for herbs and spices and intermittent arbors with climbing vines and flowers.

Passing a pomegranate tree, I plucked one of its large, red, leathery fruits. A few steps later, I began picking white blossoms from a henna bush, gathering them together until they had formed a beautiful bouquet. I turned, and as a young boy might give a gift to a little girl, presented the bouquet to my bride. She accepted with a soft laugh. We soon came to a bed of grass alongside a cinnamon tree. There, I spread out a blanket of soft lambskin, and we sat down.

While my new queen was enjoying the pleasing scent of the henna bouquet, I took the pomegranate between my hands and broke it open, then handed her a section.

"This is such beautiful place," she said as she took the piece of fruit and carefully nibbled at the juicy seeds. "Never have I been anywhere so lovely."

"Lovely it may be," I responded, "but it does not compare to another garden that

God has entrusted to my care. That garden, my darling, is you. You are not like a public garden without fences, open for any passerby to enjoy or abuse. Like this place, you are my own exclusive and private garden."

As she smiled up at me, I got up and walked over to a row of spices. Kneeling down, I picked an assortment of nard, saffron, calamus, and aloes. I collected a few of the hardened resin tears from nearby frankincense and myrrh trees, along with some bark scraped from the cinnamon tree. I brought my treasures back and laid them before my queen.

"All of these, my darling, are good for healing, preserving life or arousing the palate," I explained. "The scent of each is somewhat demure, almost unnoticeable until it is crushed, cut, or bruised. Take, for instance, this delicate purple flower."

I held it out before her, pleased to see her keen interest. "This is called saffron. Do you see these three small, bright red stigmas coming from the middle of the flower? These threadlike strands are separated from the flower and then dried. They compose the sole component of the saffron spice. If I were to cup my hands, it would take about seventy-five thousand of these flowers to produce enough saffron to fill them. As beautiful as the flowers appear, they must be destroyed in order to extract from them that which is priceless. By weight, this is the world's most expensive spice."

I gathered the spices together in my hands and ground them between my palms. I held the crushed bits up to her nose. She breathed in a deep breath of its pleasing fragrance.

"Delightful!" she responded. "But it is sad, what you say."

"Is it?" I asked. "I have been observing and learning from you, my darling. I have seen you in difficult circumstances. I have seen you bruised. I have seen you hurt. I have seen you mistreated. I have seen injustices obstruct the path of your life. But I have also seen your patience and your determination to maintain a quiet innocence. I have seen your longsuffering, your forbearance, your forgiving ways, and your compassion. I have observed the comfort and the encouragement you give to others. I have admired these pleasing virtues, each one manifest in your life as a result of the ordeals you have suffered. Like the fragrance from these wounded spices, these virtues are most precious to me and accompany you wherever you go."

Once more, I looked at the pomegranate. "You may not be aware, but like this pomegranate, there is a hidden part of you that is so full of life that you never cease to provide me with continual encouragement."

I stood up again and offered her my hand. "There is one more thing I must show you," I said.

Leaving the blanket and our food, I escorted her to the centermost part of the garden. There, I approached a large circular stone which was perfectly fitted to rest atop several others. As I removed the stone, a spring of gushing, flowing water began spilling over in four directions. Its flow coursed through the entire garden, finding small canals and rivulets to water every living thing.

"This is my Eden," I said. "As in the paradise that Adam and Eve roamed, with its fountainhead that gave birth to four mighty rivers—this is my re-creation of that blessed place. The headwaters of this spring come from the heights of Lebanon, representing heaven itself. This sealed fountain, the source of life to all living things here, is what you, my darling, are to me!"

POINTS TO CONSIDER

A spring is the source of flowing, living water. Solomon's bride was a spring—but a spring sealed. This means that although she had within herself living water and the ability to satisfy the thirst of others, that water was restricted and did not flow out to anyone, anytime, anywhere. Only when the guardian of the garden lifted the seal would the fountains within her flow freely.

To find the meaning of this, we need only look at Jesus, for he was a spring that was sealed.

Although Jesus is the source of living water, that water is only available to those for whom the Father lifts the seal. Take, for example, the man whom Jesus healed at the pool of Bethesda in John 5. He had been ill for thirty-eight years. *Bethesda* means "flowing water." On the day Jesus came, there lay a multitude of those who were sick, blind, lame, and withered, all waiting for the moving of the waters in the pool. They hoped that if the waters began to flow, they could step in and be healed.

Passing through one of the five porticoes surrounding the pool, Jesus must have paused for a moment and gazed out over the multitudes, all of whom were in need of some kind of healing. Then, proceeding toward the pool, stepping over and side-stepping body after pathetic body, he came to *this* man and asked him, "Do you wish to get well?"

Of course the man wanted to get well! But why did Jesus ask this question to only one solitary man? As the Great Physician, he was capable of healing all at the pool that day. He could have caused a spectacular scene and catapulted his popularity and fame to star status in a single moment. He certainly could have healed everyone. But he didn't. Why?

The answer is that Jesus was a sealed spring. He was the *real* Bethesda. He was the real flowing and living water, but he did not determine where that water flowed. His Father did.

Jesus often spoke about doing only those things he saw the Father doing, or speaking only those things he heard the Father speaking.

Therefore Jesus answered and was saying to them, "Truly, truly, I say to you, the Son can do nothing of Himself, unless it is something He sees the Father doing; for whatever the Father does, these things the Son also does in like manner." (John 5:19)

For I did not speak on My own initiative, but the Father Himself who sent Me has given me a commandment what to say and what to speak. I know that His commandment is eternal life; therefore the things I speak, I speak just as the Father has told me. (John 12:49–50)

Do you not believe that I am in the Father and the Father is in Me? The words that I say to you I do not speak on my own initiative, but the Father abiding in Me does His works. (John 14:10)

Why did Jesus heal only that one man that day? It was because the Father who dwelt within Jesus *as* Spirit, *in* Christ's spirit, was showing and telling his Son, "This is the man, my Son, whom I want you to heal today."

Jesus healed that man not because he needed healing more than the others, nor because he had more faith than the others, nor because he had more potential for the kingdom than the others. He healed that man because Jesus lived in total obedience to his Father. The Father lifted the seal that day, the living water flowed, and the man was healed.

In the Song of Solomon, the streams feeding the garden spring, which Solomon compared to his bride, flowed down from Lebanon. In Revelation, we see "a river of water of life, clear as crystal, coming down from the throne of God and of the Lamb" that waters the heavenly city, the New Jerusalem—the bride of Christ—with water that is alive (Revelation 22:1).

The bride in the Song is both Solomon's sealed fountain and his locked garden. In the beginning of chapter 5, we see him coming into his garden, gathering "my" myrrh along with "my" balsam, eating from "my" honeycomb and "my" honey, drinking from "my" wine and "my" milk. The king came into his garden, his bride, and with unrestrained enjoyment gratified and pleasured himself with all of her delightful fruits! Love had reached its climax. The two of them had became physically one once more.

The honey and the milk mentioned in chapter 5, verse 1, remind us of the land of Canaan, which the Lord gave the Israelites as their inheritance. It was a land "flowing with milk and honey." It was called "the Promised Land," "the good land," and an assortment of other names, but it was also called "*Beulah* Land," which means "married" (Isaiah 62:4). God's people were to become one with the land. They were to enjoy all of its precious riches. As the Book of Deuteronomy describes the land, it was:

> …a land of brooks of water, of fountains and springs, flowing forth in the valleys and hills; a land of wheat and barley, of vines and fig trees and pomegranates, a land of olive oil and honey; a land where you will eat food without scarcity, in which you will not lack anything; a land whose stones are iron, and out of whose hills you can dig copper. When you have eaten and are satisfied, you shall bless the Lord your God for the good land which He has given you. (Deuteronomy 8:7–10)

But Canaan was only a picture for Israel, and for us, of Christ who is our inheritance. He is our "good land." He is our inheritance, and God wants us to possess and enjoy all of him.

In the picture that God provides us of Solomon and his bride, we see that not only is Christ our inheritance (with all that he is and all that belongs to him), but we are *his* inheritance also. Solomon said to his bride, "I have eaten my honeycomb and my honey; I have drunk my wine and my milk." She was, to him, his land of milk and honey. She was, to him, his Promised Land.

As the two are lost in the rapture of the union of soul and body, a delightful approval bursts forth in the Song, once again from an omnipotent third party—representing God, the Father—who sanctions their marriage bliss:

"Eat, friends; drink and imbibe deeply, O lovers."

THOUGHTS/PRAYERS

You know who the king is in this story: Solomon. And you know that Solomon's private garden and sealed spring was his bride. You also know that Solomon is a type or representation of Jesus. That means that Jesus's private garden and sealed spring is *you!* He is your inheritance, and you are his. You are Jesus's Promised Land!

Now would be a good time to invite him into his garden and allow him to enjoy all of its fruits.

Lord Jesus, I am your garden. My heart, all I have, and all I am belongs to you. Come into your garden. Water me with a fresh touch of your Spirit. Enjoy what is yours. Be pleased with the fruit that you see growing in my life. Plant new seeds that will bear even more fruit for you to enjoy. Make me your sealed spring. Teach me to respond to your voice, your leading, and your impulses so that the living water in me will be released into the lives of others. Lord, you are so good. Thank you that I am your inheritance, your Promised Land. Thank you for the work you are doing in my life!

"What is written here makes one think of marriage, but what is meant is the union of the human soul with God."

ST. GREGORY OF NYSSA, FOURTH CENTURY

Loving the King with Abandon

SONG OF SONGS, CHAPTER 4

"Awake, O north wind,
And come, wind of the south;
Make my garden breathe out fragrance,
Let its spices be wafted abroad
May my beloved come into his garden
And eat its choice fruits!"
Song of Songs 4:16

"I have come into my garden, my sister, my bride;
I have gathered my myrrh along with my balsam
I have eaten my honeycomb and my honey;
I have drunk my wine and my milk."

"Eat, friends; drink and imbibe deeply, O lovers."

SONG OF SONGS 5:1

I closed the stone seal, and we returned to our shaded blanket.

We sat down. My queen took my hand, looked me in the eyes, and said, "My king and my husband, if my love for you truly makes you as alive as you say, it is unconscious on my part. All that I give to you comes so naturally. It is a pure response to the love you have given to me. I respond to you as these trees and plants respond to the waters from the spring, and like them, my love for you only continues to grow.

"You overwhelm me, again, by the words of love that flow like this living stream from my king's lips. It seems to me beyond reason and comprehension that I could be life itself to you, for I have been completely unaware of all the virtues and beauty that you see in me.

"But there is more I must say, my king.

"In what has seemed like such a short time that we have been together, I have experienced the different seasons of love—the springtime in which all is budding and alive, as it is here with you today, but also the cold winter in the periods of your absence. In those times, I have felt like a tree with fallen leaves, when all of its twisted shapes and branches are exposed. In those times, I have wanted to hide what was beneath the surface in my life. I felt as if I had no outward beauty at all, but as your presence came and went, so too did my beauty come and go."

"I know of what you speak," I interrupted, "but though it was my being with you and my displays of affection that first drew you to me and awakened love in your heart, I needed to know if you would still love me in the absence of those things. Would I find a heart that truly loved me in return, not only because of the gifts and benefits it received—a heart that would continue to love even in their absence?"

My words seemed to quiet her and draw her into reflection. "I chose you," I said softly, "because I believed that you could see the unseen, that you would not be spoiled by the luxury of your surroundings nor even by the faithfulness of my presence. I knew that many times I would have to leave you, and I knew that the comforts of the palace and of the world cannot long comfort anyone. Sometimes, the only thing you will have to keep you surviving is the belief that out there somewhere, I will return to you."

"That is a test I hope I have passed," she responded. "In love's immaturity, I became addicted to the wonderful feelings that were aroused by your intoxicating presence. But I do not just love you for those moments. I hope you know that now."

Pausing momentarily, she tenderly toyed with a single shield from the necklace that I had given her. Then she continued, "My love for you will remain steadfast regardless, even in times when it will require pure faith alone."

A gentle, warm breeze began to blow through the garden, waving the flowers in unison. My queen wrapped her arms around my neck and looked intently into my eyes. "I do not know what waits around life's next bend, but this I do know: you have captured me with your love. So awake, O chilly north wind; come, balmy wind from the south! Come, bad times; come, good times. It does not matter. It is not about me and what I want. May I cease completely from letting my emotions be tossed about on the sea of circumstances. I want my love for you to flourish under any conditions."

She lowered her voice and spoke in my ear. "O wind, make my garden breathe out fragrance. Let its spices be wafted abroad. Come, my beloved, into your garden. It all belongs to you. Eat of all its choice fruits."

I responded hastily to her invitation for love. We both began to strip off our clothes, dropped to the ground upon the soft lambskin blanket, and made passionate love together. She gave herself to me with abandon.

In the afterglow of our ecstasy, as I was still breathing heavily in short puffs and bursts, I said to my love, "I have come into my garden, my sister, my bride. I have gathered my myrrh along with my balsam. I have eaten my honeycomb and my honey. I have drunk my wine and my milk."

As we lay there together in the open air, both deeply satisfied, we suddenly became aware of a soft melody coming from nowhere, riding upon the breeze. It seemed as if a heavenly chorus was singing over us with great delight, sanctioning our marriage bliss: "Eat, friends; drink and imbibe deeply, O lovers."

POINTS TO CONSIDER

In everything give thanks; for this is God's will for you in Christ Jesus. (1 Thessalonians 5:18)

By this time in their relationship, the bride had gone through good times and bad. There had been springtime and winter, times of knowing her bridegroom's nearness and times of knowing separation. She had been to the heights with him and had been led down through those places where the lions roar and the leopards prowl. But now, at this stage of her growth in love, the many seasons and circumstances of her life were met with a single response: "Awake, O north wind, and come, wind of the south."

Spiritually, the bride was beckoning the Holy Spirit and inviting the winds—the cold, biting winds of the north, as well as the warm, balmy winds from the south— to stir a pleasing fragrance in her that would be a delight to the one she had come to love. She had arrived at a point where she saw that outward circumstances did not matter. She had grown beyond loving him in the good times but retreating or pouting in the bad. She had grown confident enough in his love that she could say, "Whatever circumstances may come my way, I will receive them with open arms, and my love for you will not change. It is not about me or what I want anymore. I know that you love me, no matter the season. Through the wind of your Holy Spirit living in me, I can flourish under any conditions."

This is the attitude we see in the apostle Paul.

For I have learned to be content in whatever circumstances I am. I know how to get along with humble means, and I also know how to live in prosperity; in any and every circumstance I have learned the secret of being filled and going hungry, both of having abundance and suffering need. I can do all things through Him who strengthens me. (Philippians 4:11–13)

Who will separate us from the love of Christ? Will tribulation, or distress, or persecution, or famine, or nakedness, or peril or sword?... But in all these things we overwhelmingly conquer through Him who loved us. For I am convinced that neither death, nor life, nor angels, nor principalities, nor things present, nor things to come, nor powers, nor height, nor depth, nor any other created thing, will be able to separate us from the love of God, which is in Christ Jesus our Lord." (Romans 8:35, 37–39)

Have we yet come to see that *everything* that happens in our lives passes first through the hands of a loving, sovereign God—by his will and with his permission—and is exactly what we need?

And... have we learned to give thanks?

It does not come naturally to us to see pain, suffering, loss, and difficulty as originating from a God who is supposed to be madly in love with us. It is even a greater stretch to give thanks. But what are our options? Do we blame the devil (who gets far too much credit) or the messenger (that ungrateful employer, that selfish friend, that disappointing spouse) for the bad things that come our way? Or do we say, "Wait a minute! Even the devil is under God's authority, and, as in the case of Job, cannot bring anything against me without first being granted permission. Therefore, what is happening in my life *right now* (unless it involves outright sin on my part) must be the perfect expression of the will of God and is for my ultimate good."

What we sometimes think has come directly from the enemy may have come to us from the Lord of life himself in order to lovingly capture some stray part of our lives that has not yet fully come under his control.

Even Joseph, when recounting to his brothers their treachery when they abandoned him in a pit and sold him to Ishmaelite traders for twenty shekels of silver (an act of betrayal which led to his imprisonment in Egypt and all kinds of suffering), could say, "As for you, you meant evil against me, but God meant it for good in order to bring about this present result, to preserve many people alive" (Genesis 50:20).

This is a milestone in Christian maturity to which we can all aspire: to bring to God a heart of thanksgiving *for all things.*

But there is more. This goes deeper.

So far, we have only been considering outward circumstances. But what about our private, inner lives with the Lord? The same principle applies.

Can we say these words with Paul?

I have learned to be content in whatever [spiritual] circumstances I am. I know how to get along with humble means [times of spiritual dryness; times when I do not "feel" that the Lord is near], and I also know how to live in prosperity [times of spiritual blessing and enjoyment; times when I have a clear sense of his presence]; in any and every [spiritual] circumstance [season in my life] I have learned the secret of being filled and going hungry, both of having abundance and suffering need. I can do all things through Him who strengthens me. (Philippians 4:11–13)

Bringing this down to a very practical level, how does this apply to our prayer times? If God chooses to bless us with a sense of his presence, speak to us, or touch us in some way, don't we naturally walk away from that experience giving thanks? But what if he chooses to withhold his presence, to not speak to us or give us any sense that the time we devoted to him has any value or has made any difference? Can we receive that, as well, as coming from him—*and give thanks?*

Will we keep coming back?

Sometimes, God hides himself in order to rouse us from our spiritual laziness. At other times, he hides himself to see if we will remain faithful in coming to him even if there appears to be no spiritual blessing or benefit at all.

Coming to God with a heart that seeks nothing from him but *only to please him,* that is the mark of faithfulness.

Lingering before our Lord, even after we have said all there is to say; waiting before him in respectful, worshipful silence; forgetting the past and leaving the future in his hands; living with him in the embrace of the present—these are all fragrances that are surely pleasing to our Beloved.

"Awake, O north wind, and come, wind of the south."

THOUGHTS/PRAYERS

Let this be our attitude and prayer: "Awake, O north wind, and come, wind of the south. Make my garden breathe out fragrance, let its spices be wafted abroad."

His Desire Is for Me ⁓ 123

Only the Holy Spirit can perfect this kind of steadfastness and faithfulness in our lives and produce a love in our hearts for God that flourishes under any conditions. This is our hope!

And hope does not disappoint, because the love of God has been poured out within our hearts through the Holy Spirit who was given to us. (Romans 5:5)

Agony of the Night

SONG OF SONGS, CHAPTER 5

"I was asleep but my heart was awake.
A voice! My beloved was knocking:
'Open to me, my sister, my darling,
My dove, my perfect one!
For my head is drenched with dew,
My locks with the damp of the night.'
'I have taken off my dress,
How can I put it on again?
I have washed my feet,
How can I dirty them again?'
My beloved extended his hand through the opening,
And my feelings were aroused for him.
I arose to open to my beloved;
And my hands dripped with myrrh,
And my fingers with liquid myrrh,
On the handles of the bolt.
I opened to my beloved,
But my beloved had turned away and had gone!
My heart went out to him as he spoke
I searched for him but I did not find him;
I called him but he did not answer me."

SONG OF SONGS 5:2–6

There was yet a side of the king that I had not seen before. One afternoon he came to me, telling me that he was troubled and planned to leave the palace on his own that night and go to a secluded olive orchard across the Kidron Valley to pray. This seemed strange, but I did not question him further.

At dusk, donning a hooded cloak so that he would not be recognized, the king left the palace in secret and made his way to the orchard. Many matters concerning the kingdom weighed heavily on his mind that night, not the least of which (I found out later) was me.

My love had brought him deep satisfaction, but he still had one concern. Was I showing too much confidence that my love for him could never be shaken? Was there a principle, inherent in nature and written into the very fabric of the universe itself, that like those seeds in his garden, my love would need to survive the test of death before it could really prove to be unfailing? Would my own love need to be tested more before I would come to realize that such a pure love could only come from God and was not within my grasp as a mere mortal?

Perhaps another man would not even have thought such things, or desired such pure love. But my king was not like other men!

When he arrived at the orchard, he fell to his knees beside a large rock, near an old olive press, and began to pray. It was a long, lonely night. With sorrow and agony, he wrestled with one who ruled a kingdom far greater than that of Israel, even with the Lord God Almighty.

The king lost track of time. By the time he finally emerged from the orchard, it was just before dawn. Returning to the palace, he approached my room. His raven-black hair and his clothes dripped with the dew of the night.

I had retired earlier, but I was awakened when I heard his loud knock at my door. "Open to me, my sister, my darling, my dove, my perfect one!" said the king. "For my head is drenched with dew, and my locks with the damp of the night."

I could sense the overwhelming desire he had to be with me.

Yet, I had not expected his call at this late hour, and I hesitated. I did not really want to open to him. The memory of my garden pledge to love him under any conditions flashed through my mind, but I quickly dismissed the thought. This was not a test of love—it was simply a matter of courtesy and convenience! *What can I say to him?* I thought. Clearing my throat, yet wondering if he might see through my feeble excuse, I responded, "I have taken off my dress. How can I put it on again? I have washed my feet. How can I dirty them again?"

I could not entirely hide the irritation in my voice. My beloved had come to me again, but this time it was not as the winsome king, nor as the apple tree among the trees of the forest. Nor had he come as the gallant gazelle, the glad groom, or the manly mountaineer—not even as the gentle gardener. This time he came to me at an hour and in a form of which I did not approve.

He knocked again, seeking admittance, but I gave him no response. Finally, he inserted his hand through the hole by the door to reach around for the latch and open it himself. Seeing his hand faintly in the dark, I finally aroused myself, slowly got up, and walked to the door, only to find the bolt dripping with liquid myrrh. When I opened the door, he was gone.

My conscience was smitten. I recalled in an instant the words of young love that had rolled from my own lips: "Draw me after you, and let us run together." Had I been so naive? Did I think my desires would only be answered by the king taking me to the mountaintops? Did I want him only for the times of smelling the flowers in the countryside or in his garden? How did I not realize that running together meant not only hearing the voice of the turtledoves and seeing the vines in blossom, but also sharing with him in his times of trouble and suffering?

I raced down the hall searching for him, but I did not find him. I called out to him, but there was no answer.

I quickly returned to my chamber. In a rush to pursue him, I wrapped myself in a robe and grabbed a veil to throw over my head. *Maybe he returned to that orchard across the valley,* I thought to myself. *I will go there to look for him.*

POINTS TO CONSIDER

…that I may know Him and the power of His resurrection and the fellowship of His sufferings, being conformed to His death; in order that I may attain to the resurrection from the dead. (Philippians 3:10–11)

In the earlier stages of love, the maiden's earnest desire was for the king to "draw me after you, and let us run together" (Song of Songs 1:4). This is also our desire, for the Lord to draw us after him. But as young Christians, when we pray this kind of prayer, do we really have any idea what we are asking? In our naivety, do we think he will answer those prayers by taking us with him only to the mountaintops and high places, by giving us only seasons of springtime? In those times of consecration when we give ourselves to the Lord, we must realize that we are committing to follow him anywhere—even if it is to the cross and to the place of suffering.

This portrayal of King Solomon calls to mind Christ's hours of darkness that night in Gethsemane when his disciples, like the bride in the song, were summoned to join him to watch and pray—but in their drowsiness, they did not respond.

Following the Last Supper and one final hymn with his disciples, the night of our Lord's agony began at about 8:00 p.m. He left the upper room with the disciples and led them through the narrow streets of Jerusalem, across the double-tiered bridge spanning the Kidron Valley to the Mount of Olives and the garden of Gethsemane. Then, leaving the eleven, Jesus walked ahead of them through a grove of trees to a spot where he collapsed to the ground and began crying out, in loud cries, to his Father. There, he wrestled with the Father—his will pitted against the Father's will—and the conflict was over a cup.

That cup was the Father's will. There in Gethsemane (which means "an oil press"), Jesus, like an olive crushed in the oil press, poured out his soul and grappled with anguish until his own will surrendered and he laid hold of the Father's will.

After returning to the disciples a third time to rouse them, with his hair matted with sweat, his forehead and cheeks streaked with sweat and blood from ruptured vessels in his face, he had finally embraced the cup the Father was asking him to drink. It was the cup of humiliation, pain, abandonment, wrath, and death—and he drank it all with dignity. His was a matchless example of how to embrace and accept the crosses God gives us to bear!

Finally, the soldiers came with their lanterns and torches, along with the betrayer, and at about midnight, they bound Jesus as a criminal and whisked him away to the palace of the high priest, adjacent to the temple. Already exhausted, there in the judgment hall Christ endured a mock trial consisting of ridicule, an unjust string of lies, false accusations, and crazed hatred and taunts from a pack of religious fools.

He was spat upon. He endured a brutal beating. He was punched in the face, struck with rods, made fun of, and finally led away to Pilate. From there, he was taken to his appointment with the nails that would impale him to a tree.

This is the image of the one whom we see knocking at the queen's door—the one whose head was drenched with dew and whose locks dripped with the damp of the night.

Did the Father have the power to spare Jesus from this horrific ordeal? Of course he did. But because of an eternal covenant, agreed upon between them before the dawning of time, Jesus had to die (Hebrews 13:20). This was all part of redemption's price tag. It was the ultimate act of obedience so that, through the death of a perfect man, the spotless Lamb of God, sinners could be redeemed and live.

Not all of us will be called to endure physical suffering at the hands of others as our Lord did, nor as did countless martyrs, nor as untold numbers of those living in hostile lands have suffered—but some will.

Suffering is part of our destiny as Christians. Without it, how could we ever feel true compassion for others? How could we ever comfort those in pain and crisis, unless we had found comfort in such times ourselves?

Blessed be the God and Father of our Lord Jesus Christ, the Father of mercies and God of all comfort, who comforts us in all our affliction so that we will be able to comfort those who are in any affliction with the comfort with which we ourselves are comforted by God. For just as the sufferings of Christ are ours in abundance, so also our comfort is abundant through Christ. But if we are afflicted it is for your comfort and salvation; or if we are comforted it is for your comfort. (2 Corinthians 1:3–6)

We are afflicted in every way, but not crushed; perplexed, but not despairing; persecuted, but not forsaken; struck down, but not destroyed; always carrying about in the body the dying of Jesus, so that the life of Jesus also may be manifested in our body. For we who live are constantly being delivered over to death for Jesus' sake, so that the life of Jesus also may be manifested in our mortal flesh. So that death works in us, but life in you. (2 Corinthians 4:8–12)

THOUGHTS/PRAYERS

If you ever want to have a ministry of life to others, there is only one way to get there: embrace the one knocking on the door of your heart, whose head is drenched in dew and whose fingers drip with liquid myrrh from the agony of the night.

He will come knocking. It is not with the purpose to destroy you, but to make you richer.

The deep needs of a damaged world await a comforter to come to them.

That comforter could be you—giving comfort to others with the comfort which you have received from God in your times of trial and suffering.

The epic poem by Watchman Nee, "Let Us Contemplate the Grapevine," leaves us with these thoughts to reflect upon:

Not by gain our life is measured,
But by what we've lost 'tis scored;
'Tis not how much wine is drunken,
But how much has been outpoured;

For the strength of love e'er standeth
In the sacrifice we bear;
He who has the greatest suff'ring
Ever has the most to share.

Wounded by the Watchman

SONG OF SONGS, CHAPTER 5

"I opened to my beloved,
But my beloved had turned away and had gone!
My heart went out to him as he spoke
I searched for him but I did not find him;
I called him but he did not answer me.
The watchmen who make the rounds in the city found me,
They struck me and wounded me;
The guardsmen of the walls took away my shawl from me."

SONG OF SONGS 5:6–7

Leaving the palace on my own, I stepped out into the dark streets of Jerusalem. Surprisingly, there were still people milling about at that early morning hour. I heard the raucous laughter of drunken men. I saw beggars and homeless men curled up in doorways. Fear moved my feet quickly. I pulled my shawl down closer to my eyes.

Hurriedly rounding a corner, I ran right into a group of watchmen who were making their rounds in the city. Bouncing off one of them, I lost my balance and fell to the ground. Awkwardly, I tried to get up.

"What is this pretty little lady doing out by herself so late at night? One of the town whores returning from a tryst?" jeered one of the watchmen. They encircled me, trapping me up against a wall.

I was terrified.

Before I could speak, one of them raised his arm and delivered a sharp blow to the side of my face with the back of his hand. Reeling from the blow, I staggered and fell into the arms of another of my mockers. Whirling me around, he too struck me on the face, this time drawing blood from the corner of my mouth. Emboldened, they continued to mock and insult me. They were rough and cruel—and without reason. I was passed from one to the other, and each inflicted his own blow.

My mind spun with horror. What more would they do? Would they molest me? Rape me? Or even kill me? I was totally at their mercy and unable to defend myself.

"God, have mercy," I whispered as I received another strike to the head and collapsed to the ground.

Finally, they were finished. They left me in a cowering mass with my arms trembling, covering my head to protect myself from further beating. The roar of their laughter filled my ears as they walked off into the night.

Not many paces behind the watchmen, a few of the guardsmen from the city walls were returning home from their shift. They had slowed to watch the taunting and the beating. Assuming I was a prostitute, one of them grabbed my shawl and ripped it from my head as he passed by. Looking back, he sneered and shouted, "Let this be a lesson to you! No respectable woman walks the streets at night alone, especially with a robe like that, unless she is trying to fetch a high price and sell her body for profit. Be off now! Go to your home or wherever it is you stay. Let people see your bleeding face so that your shame will become public and no longer remain hidden."

Wounded and bruised, I could not force myself to get up. I could only lie there on the ground—for how long, I do not know. No one else passed by. With my ear to the pavement, the only sound I could hear was that of my heart pounding frantically in my chest.

What just happened? I thought. How could I have been so completely misunderstood? Did these men not recognize me and know that I was married to the king? If they had known who it was they mistreated so, they would have known that surely they would be put to death for such actions! How could this wounding, ridicule, and scorn have come from the very ones who should have been my protectors?

Finally, I staggered to my feet, wincing with pain. I wiped the blood from my mouth. My head throbbed. My body ached all over.

Stumbling forward, I tried to resume the search for my beloved but quickly realized that I was in need of help. Regaining a sense of where I was, I looked around. Across the street was a house where a number of the daughters of Jerusalem resided. I thought to myself, *Maybe they can help me.*

POINTS TO CONSIDER

The watchmen in this section of the Song represent spiritual leaders within the body of Christ.

God's intention is to place those to whom he lends his spiritual authority as lights, guides, and protectors for his people. However, in his mysterious ways, this authority falls upon two types of persons—both with their own lineage, both anointed by God, but with two distinctly different manners of wielding that authority.

These types are seen in two men from the Bible. One was a Benjamite. The other came from the tribe of Judah. One started out well and showed great promise, but in the end was remembered only as a mad king. The other, although he failed at times, was remembered as a man after God's own heart and the greatest king of Israel. It was from his loins that the Messiah would come. One threw spears, while the other did not return the favor. One became jealous and saw his rival as a threat to his empire. The other laid no claim to the kingdom at all, but saw it as a gift. One was King Saul; the other, King David.

The watchmen in this portion of the song represent those leaders in the lineage of King Saul.

In his love, God may place you within the "kingdom" of someone who does not recognize you for who you are. Such a one can even become obsessed with throwing spears at you, or hunting you down like a fugitive to destroy you, although you may have helped defeat his enemies, stabilize his kingdom, and serenade him with your sweet song.

Cruel as it may seem, this was David's preparation for the throne. His was an internship of pain, sorrow, and loss of reputation, *at the hands of one who was once anointed by God and was now ruler of the kingdom!*

In the beginning, Saul had ruled well. Later, he found himself facing a competitor. That competitor was no more than a young lad—but there was some weakness in Saul. He was incapable of embracing the thought that there would be a good man, a future king, to take his place. Saul became eaten up with jealousy.

During those dark days when David was forced to flee from him, Saul twisted the truth about his perceived enemy. He did everything in his power to turn everyone against David. He ran David's name into the ground until it became a byword. Women within the kingdom who wanted to frighten their little children would say, "Behave yourself, or you will end up like David!"

Persecution hurts—and can even be devastating—no matter its source. But persecution's real anguish comes when it is inflicted by the hand of a leader—a *Christian leader,* one who is supposed to be representing God and one whom you have lovingly served.

Not only was Solomon's bride wounded, but the guardsmen of the walls took away her her shawl. They tried to expose her in front of others. Thinking she must be guilty of some heinous sin, they maligned her and broadcast her supposed failure, making it public news.

David lamented this same treatment concerning the persecution he suffered at the hands of his adversaries: "For they have persecuted him whom You Yourself have smitten, and they tell of the pain of those whom You have wounded" (Psalm 69:26).

Leaving the watchmen and the guardsmen, concealing her tender bruises and the piercing wounds they had inflicted, the queen sought help from the daughters of Jerusalem.

THOUGHTS/PRAYERS

If you had been the queen in this story, what would have been paramount in your mind to say to those daughters of Jerusalem? Would you have poured out the story of the merciless beating you had just received?

What if God were to place a Saul-like authority figure in your life who tried to destroy you, to malign you, or to inflict unsolicited pain upon you? And what if this was done in the midst of your devastating loss of the presence of Christ and your sincere desire to find him again? What would you feel compelled to talk about?

Would you wear your hurt on your sleeve? Would you be so angry about the mistreatment you had suffered that you would want to retaliate? Would you attempt to solicit the sympathy of others and go after your attackers, returning spear for spear, justifying your behavior, and explaining how you had been wronged? This would be only reasonable… if you too had the heart of a Saul.

Nothing can prepare a Christian for the kind of suffering represented by what this maiden experienced. It came totally unexpectedly. It was unjustified, cruel, and hurtful. But this is the kind of test that God will allow his servants to go through to see whether they belong to the lineage of a King Saul or a King David. The test will determine whether *you* will become a great king or just another madman.

Perhaps you are, in this moment, in the position of being wounded or attacked. If not, it may be something you have experienced in the past or that still awaits you in the future. Whatever your case, when you see this kind of behavior—when a so-called Christian leader appears to have gone mad and mercilessly goes after a fellow believer in an attempt to destroy him or her—do not be surprised. God may just be preparing another in the line of King David for a royal assignment. Pray for them both, but especially for the one dodging the spears. You may have been given a part to play in seeing another person after God's own heart raised up to lead God's people in the ways of the Great Shepherd. And if that person is you? Take heart! Consider it an honor. For God is working his purposes in your life, even as he did in the life of his own beloved Son.

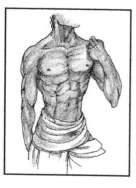

A Description of the Beloved

SONG OF SONGS, CHAPTER 5

"I adjure you, O daughters of Jerusalem,
    If you find my beloved,
    As to what you will tell him:
    For I am lovesick."

"What kind of beloved is your beloved,
    O most beautiful among women?
What kind of beloved is your beloved,
    That thus you adjure us?"

"My beloved is dazzling and ruddy,
Outstanding among ten thousand.
    His head is like gold, pure gold;
    His locks are like clusters of dates
        And black as a raven.
        His eyes are like doves
        Beside streams of water,
            Bathed in milk,
        And reposed in their setting.
His cheeks are like a bed of balsam,
    Banks of sweet-scented herbs;
        His lips are lilies
    Dripping with liquid myrrh.
    His hands are rods of gold
        Set with beryl;

His abdomen is carved ivory
Inlaid with sapphires.
His legs are pillars of alabaster
Set on pedestals of pure gold;
His appearance is like Lebanon
Choice as the cedars.
His mouth is full of sweetness
And he is wholly desirable.
This is my beloved and this is my friend,
O daughters of Jerusalem."

SONG OF SONGS 5:8–16

Casting a fearful glance over my shoulder at the dark city street, I knocked loudly on their door. Then I stepped back a few paces into the shadows to conceal the bruises and dishevelment I had received at the hands of the watchmen. It seemed an age before the door opened to reveal a half-dozen maidens huddled in their nightclothes in the entryway. Squinting into the darkness, they took a moment before they finally recognized me. "What brings you here at this late hour, most beautiful among women?" they asked, their voices betraying how greatly they were perplexed by my unexpected visit at this hour of the night.

At that moment I made a choice. I determined that I would not divulge to them the incident with the watchmen and the guardsmen. I would not tell them of my nightmarish encounter. I did not want to invoke their sympathy nor incite their rage—nor possibly tarnish the reputation of those who gave loyal service to the king. I veiled myself more closely before I stepped into the light. I only hoped that they would not perceive the hellish ordeal I had just been through.

"My beloved has gone," I replied. "I went out to look for him but have not been able to find him. Please, come with me and help me. And if you do find him, you must tell him that I love him."

"You tremble as you speak," they answered. "What deep love moves you to seek your beloved at such an hour? He must be wonderful indeed! We will help you search for him, but first, describe him so that we may know what kind of beloved is your beloved," they responded.

"How will I describe him?" I pondered aloud.

I opened my mouth but did not speak of the one who, a few hours earlier, had come to me with his locks dripping with the dew of the night. Instead, I spoke of him whom I had always known and loved. Once I began speaking of him, it seemed that my spirit began to rise out of the pit of despair. Healing began to flow. Well-springs of life began to break forth within me again.

"My beloved is dazzling and ruddy, outstanding among ten thousand. His head is like gold, pure gold. His locks are like clusters of dates and black as a raven," I began.

One of the daughters asked, "You mean ruddy like King David?"

"Yes," I responded. "Like the greatest king of Israel, King David—the harp-playing, giant-killing, singer-poet, shepherd king."

They smiled and nodded, and I continued.

"You will also recognize him by his dark and peaceful eyes. They are like those of doves beside streams of water, bathed in milk. To gaze at his cheeks is like receiving the healing properties that come from a bed of balsam, and his lips are as the deep scarlet of the lilies."

"So handsome," one of the maidens whispered. "Continue, dear sister."

"He will have gold rings, set in beryl, upon his fingers. His head, his generous and giving hands, and his feet are all as gold, representing the very nature of God. To me, my beloved is flawless in all his ways, in all his thoughts, in whatever he touches, and wherever he decides to go."

As his image came more and more clearly to my mind, I became even more enlivened, and their eyes shone with my joy.

"At the center of his being, he has an inner strength and royalty. His belly is as ivory—the very substance of the throne upon which he sits—inlaid with bright sapphires, as blue as the heavens. Unlike the diminutive alabaster bottles and vases in which we place our treasures of costly perfumes and ointments, his legs are as pillars of alabaster set on pedestals of pure gold. He is tall and strong in appearance, as the cedars of Lebanon. And when he speaks, his words are like the most beautiful music ever composed. There is gentleness and sweetness to his words. They have the ability to still the deepest troubles of the heart."

I smiled as I finished, though there was pain in the smile. My own words had increased my longing to find him—but they had also brought peace. Lifting my chin, I finished by pronouncing:

"He is wholly desirable. This is my beloved, and this is my friend."

POINTS TO CONSIDER

The bride's first words to the daughters of Jerusalem were about her beloved, not about the terrible beating she had just received. She wanted them to help her find him and to make sure he knew that she was consumed with love for him.

There is only one other person in all of Scripture who is described as ruddy, and that is King David. *Ruddy* means "reddish" and may even imply a veiled comparison to Adam, whose name means "red man." Before the fall, Adam had been made in the image of God as the original prototype for the entire human race.

Now he [David] was ruddy, with beautiful eyes and a handsome appearance. And the Lord said [to Samuel], "Arise, anoint him, for this is he." (1 Samuel 16:12)

As Saul's sanity began to waver and his aggression toward David increased, David did not attack Saul, although Saul was committed to killing David. When given an opportunity to slay his pursuer in the cave by Engedi, David refused, although his men urged him to do so:

The men of David said to him, "Behold this is the day of which the Lord said to you, 'Behold; I am about to give your enemy into your hand, and you shall do to him as it seems good to you.'" Then David arose and cut off the edge of Saul's robe secretly.

It came about afterward that David's conscience bothered him because he had cut off the edge of Saul's robe. So he said to his men, "Far be it from me because of the Lord that I should do this thing to my lord, the Lord's anointed, to stretch out my hand against him, since he is the Lord's anointed." (1 Samuel 24:4–6)

David understood that the kingdom belongs to God. It is up to God to raise or bring down kings. David refused to take that responsibility upon himself. He knew that if it was God's will that he rule the kingdom, then God would vindicate him and establish him as king.

In the queen's adulation for her husband-hero, King Solomon, she compared him first to the great king, King David. By praising Solomon instead of attacking the watchmen, she passed "the Saul test." She proved herself a follower of the man from the tribe of Judah and took her stand in the lineage of royalty whose hearts are fashioned after David—and after the one whom David called *his* Lord (Psalm 110:1).

Blessed are you when men hate you, and ostracize you, and insult you, and scorn your name as evil, for the sake of the Son of Man. (Luke 6:22)

Therefore I am well content with weaknesses, with insults, with distresses, with persecutions, with difficulties, for Christ's sake; for when I am weak, then I am strong. (2 Corinthians 12:10)

...not returning evil for evil or insult for insult, but giving a blessing instead; for you were called for the very purpose that you might inherit a blessing. (1 Peter 3:9)

At this stage in the story, Solomon's wife shows that she is worthy to be called queen:

- She could proclaim, by faith (even in the midst of an experience where the Lord seemed to have left her), that he was dazzling and the fairest among ten thousand.
- Although she appeared to have lost him, she had not lost her beauty. The daughters of Jerusalem still recognized her as the most beautiful among women, even when they saw her in a state of desperately searching for her beloved.
- Once she began to speak about her beloved, it seems as if she could not stop, and her hope was restored.
- Her description of him was not spoken *to* him, but *to* the daughters of Jerusalem. This was the word of her testimony (Revelation 12:11). Speaking the truth about him gave her strength and seems to have made him real to her once again.
- Toward the end of her description of him, she could say that he was wholly desirable and altogether lovely.
- She concluded with, "This is my beloved, and this is my friend."

THOUGHTS PRAYERS

Persecution makes some people bitter. For others, it is the path to royalty. If the Lord were to bring persecution into your life—even from the hands of those who call themselves Christians—would you be able to endure their wounds, take your anger and feelings of retribution to the cross, and come out of this test among the royal ranks of those like David and the Shulammite, who were still able to love the Lord and call him their friend?

Lord Jesus, I ask you to guard my heart and my lips from returning insult for insult and attacking those who would attack me. I want to follow the example you gave when you stood before those religious leaders at that contemptible trial the morning before you were crucified, where they lied and testified falsely against you and even beat you. You did not complain, murmur, or threaten. You accepted the cross the Father gave you, and you did it with dignity. Bring the Saul in me to that cross and give me grace that I might bless and even pray for my enemies.

Day Twenty

Knowing His Unfailing Love

SONG OF SONGS, CHAPTER 6

"Where has your beloved gone,
O most beautiful among women?
Where has your beloved turned,
That we may seek him with you?"

"My beloved has gone down to his garden,
To the beds of balsam,
To pasture his flock in the gardens
And gather lilies.
I am my beloved's and my beloved is mine,
He who pastures his flock among the lilies."

"You are as beautiful as Tirzah, my darling,
As lovely as Jerusalem,
As awesome as an army with banners.
Turn your eyes away from me,
For they have confused me;
Your hair is like a flock of goats
That have descended from Gilead.
Your teeth are like a flock of ewes
Which have come up from their washing,
All of which bear twins,
And not one among them has lost her young.
Your temples are like a slice of a pomegranate
Behind your veil."

SONG OF SONGS 6:1–7

His Desire Is for Me ≈ 141

"Where do you think your beloved has gone, O most beautiful among women?" inquired the maidens. "Where has your beloved turned that we may seek him with you?"

As I had been speaking of him, my mind became clear once again. Suddenly, I realized that my beloved had probably not gone back to the orchard across the valley after all. Where would he expect me to come if he knew I was looking for him? Most likely, it would not be to some unfamiliar place, but to a place with which I was well acquainted. *His garden!* Instinctively, I knew that I would find him there.

"My beloved has gone down to his garden, to the beds of balsam!" I exclaimed as the revelation burst upon me. "He must have gone there to greet the early morning light and to feed and gather lilies!"

Instantly, I was aware that this was nowhere these maidens were allowed to go, for this was the king's private garden—a place only the two of us shared. I hastily bid them good-bye, turned, and raced back to my chamber.

My composure returned on the way back to the palace. Dawn was about to break, and the approach of the light seemed to scatter the dangers of the street. By the time I arrived, a new confidence had begun to rise within me. Although my love for the king had faltered when he came unexpectedly to my room, I clutched to the hope that his love for me would not fail. I somehow knew, deep within, that if he had once promised that I was his garden and his sealed spring, it must still be so.

I was exhausted. I desperately needed some rest before I resumed my search for the king. Confident once more in his love, I knew he would not begrudge me time to prepare to meet him.

I returned to my bedchamber, and after a brief repose, I awakened. The sun was shining brightly into my room. I got up, bathed, and dressed. I sat down at my table and reached for a mirror. The bruises I had received in the night were still there. I placed some reddish powder from a small box onto my fingers and was about to rub it onto my cheeks to conceal the bruises. But then I stopped. "No," I whispered to myself. "I dare not cover them. He must see me as I am."

I arose and made my way to the garden. When I arrived, I saw the lock hanging on the gate, and the gate itself opened. I slipped inside and saw Solomon, at a distance, pruning a row of ornamental shrubs. I approached him cautiously. As I drew close, he became aware of my presence and turned to look at me.

I expected a rebuke for my rude and uncaring behavior the night before. Perhaps he would chastise me, or at least scold me. Perchance I would hear an analysis of my failures. But it was not to be so. Instead, I heard the most lovely words come from the king's lips—words that caught me completely by surprise. They were words he had spoken to me a thousand times, words I had grown to cherish, and they brought tears of joy to my eyes.

"You are beautiful, my darling," he said with a smile. "You are as beautiful as Tirzah, the ancient Canaanite city of delights. You are as lovely as Jerusalem itself, which is the joy of the whole earth! You are as awesome as an army with their banners exalted in the air, proclaiming victory."

As I stared at him, I could see tears welling up within his own eyes. He seemed overwhelmed with emotion. "Turn your eyes away," he said, with lips quivering. "Your beauty is too much for me. I cannot take it in."

He paused for a moment and then continued. He repeated the very words describing my hair, my teeth, and my temples that he had spoken on our wedding day. The repetition was as beautiful as the words themselves. Nothing had changed! His love for me was just as strong and immovable as it had been on that day. It was a love that was blind to all my faults and weaknesses, all my mistakes, ultimately, perhaps, even to all my sin.

My heart melted, once again, in complete surrender to a love which so transcended my own, a love over which I had no power for good or ill. It was as if I had begun to touch, to see, a love with currents so deep that they could neither be fathomed nor understood.

In that moment, I was convinced beyond doubt that the bond of our love was secure. Our bond was based on his unfailing love for me, not on the frailty and fickleness of my love for him.

POINTS TO CONSIDER

Sometimes, the Lord will show us something and then later take us back to see the same thing again, only from a different perspective. Sometimes we need to relearn an old lesson. And sometimes, especially after we have sinned or feel like we have failed the Lord, he will bring us back to show us again that he still loves us; that he still sees us as his dove, his darling, his perfect one; that his love is steadfast and will never fail.

In these passages, Solomon repeats to his bride the things he said to her on their wedding day: her hair is like a flock of goats, her teeth like a flock of ewes, and her temples like a slice of pomegranate. Throughout the Song of Songs there is a continual repetition of things said before, both by the bride and by the king.

- "I would lead you and bring you into the house of my mother" in chapter 8, verse 2, is a repeat of the Shulammite's desire in chapter 3, verse 4.

- "Let his left hand be under my head and his right hand embrace me" in chapter 8, verse 3, repeats another of her longings in chapter 2, verse 6.
- The king compares her eyes to "dove's eyes" in chapter 1, verse 15, and again in chapter 4, verse 1; her breasts to "two fawns" in chapter 4, verse 5, and again in chapter 7, verse 3.
- "I want you to swear, O daughters of Jerusalem, do not arouse or awaken my love until she pleases" in chapter 8, verse 4, repeats what the king said in chapters, 2, verse 7, and 3, verse 5.
- "Who is this coming up from the wilderness?" in chapter 8, verse 5, is a repeat of what is said in chapter 3, verse 6.

And all the way through the Song, the king repeatedly tells his bride how beautiful and lovely she is.

Having God take you back and show you something that you have seen before is a good thing. Take, for example, the first time you became aware of his love. Most likely, that was the day of your salvation, when the Holy Spirit convicted you of your sin, you repented, and you accepted God's free gift of salvation and saw for the first time that "God so loved the world that he sent his only Son, that whosoever believes in him [and that was you], should not perish but have everlasting life" (John 3:16).

Then, later in life, you might have received some further enlightenment. Since your initial experience of the Lord's love, after walking with him for a while, you began to notice the nagging recurrence of sin. Although you had been saved for some time, you became aware that you still had the capacity to sin. Every once in a while, one just "popped out." In that moment you saw more clearly that God not only loved you and forgave you, but that he loved you *in spite of your sins*. His blood has not only covered the sins of the past, but also the sins of the present, and it will cover the sins of the future. As a result of your experience, you gained a deeper appreciation for that love.

For it was fitting for us to have such a high priest, holy, innocent, undefiled, separated from sinners and exalted above the heavens; who does not need daily, like those high priests, to offer up sacrifices, first for His own sins, and then for the *sins* of the people, because this He did *once for all*, when he offered up Himself." (Hebrews 7:26–27, emphasis mine)

Our Lord offered himself one time—for all—never to return again to that revolting cross to bear any future sins for the human race. Redemption was finished. Your sins were paid for: past sins, present sins, and, yes, future sins. It was all a free gift.

Did God know that after you received him as your Savior you would still sometimes sin? Of course! Did that change his love for you? No. For him to love you, in spite of your sins, may have come as a surprise to you—but it was certainly no surprise to him. Through further revelation, you once again came to appreciate his love, but now at a deeper level.

Then, one day, you made a new discovery. You discovered, like Paul did, that not only are you capable of sinning, but sin actually *dwells in you*. Except for the grace of God, you are a full-blown sin factory!

> For what I am doing, I do not understand; for I am not practicing what I would like to do, but I am doing the very thing I hate. But if I do the very thing I do not want to do, I agree with the Law, confessing that the Law is good. So now, no longer am I the one doing it, but sin dwells in me. For I know that nothing good dwells in me, that is, in my flesh… I find then the principle that evil is present in me, the one who wants to do good. (Romans 7:15–18, 21)

In spite of that, *God still loves you!* About this time, like Paul, you received even more light and revelation:

> Therefore there is now no condemnation for those who are in Christ Jesus. For the law of the Spirit of life in Christ Jesus has set you free from the law of sin and of death. (Romans 8:1–2)

Now you have come to know that God not only loves you, but he loves you in spite of your *sins* and in spite of your *sin* (the very sin nature that dwells within you).

> Otherwise, He would have needed to suffer often since the foundation of the world; but now once at the consummation of the ages He has been manifested to put away *sin* by the sacrifice of Himself." (Hebrews 9:26, emphasis mine)

The message continues, more incredible with every new glimmer of understanding. He has not only put away sin but has placed you "in Christ," and in Christ, there is no condemnation. To fully comprehend this love will require the ages of eternity.

For this reason I bow my knees before the Father, from whom every family in heaven and on earth derives its name, that He would grant you, according to the riches of His glory, to be strengthened with power through His Spirit in the inner man, so that Christ may dwell in your hearts through faith, and that you, being rooted and grounded in love, may be able to comprehend with all the saints what is the breadth and length and height and depth, and to know the love of Christ which surpasses knowledge, that you may be filled up to all the fullness of God. (Ephesians 3:14–19)

As Simon Peter learned from the Lord Jesus, a follower of Christ cannot outgrow the need to be reminded, from time to time, of some of the most basic truths. He wrote, "Therefore, I will always be ready to remind you of these things even though you already know them, and have been established in the truth which is present with you. I consider it right, as long as I am in this earthly dwelling, to stir you up by way of reminder"(2 Peter 1:12–13).

This is the wonderful lesson that we can glean from this passage of the Song: as Solomon's love for his bride did not change, neither will our Lord's love for us ever change.

What a Lord! What a king! What a God!

And what a lover.

THOUGHTS/PRAYERS

Lord, thank you for your love. Thank you that it is so deep, it will take eternity to comprehend. Thank you for your patience. Thank you for all the chances you give me to learn from you. Continue to show me more and more of your love until I am convinced that it will not change. Take me back as often as you like to remind me how much you love me. I ask this, because sometimes I forget.

Increasing Love

SONG OF SONGS, CHAPTER 6

"Where has your beloved gone,
O most beautiful among women?
Where has your beloved turned,
That we may seek him with you?"

"My beloved has gone down to his garden,
To the beds of balsam,
To pasture his flock in the gardens
And gather lilies.
I am my beloved's and my beloved is mine,
He who pastures his flock among the lilies."

SONG OF SONGS 6:1–3

The maiden's initial love for the king and a believer's initial love for Christ can be summarized by Song of Songs 2:16: "My beloved is mine, and I am his." At that stage, the maiden was growing in her knowledge of the king, but by her own words, the emphasis was still on herself. She had seen many things about him, but those revelations had not yet been made a permanent part of her life.

As Christians, receiving Christ and having him come into our lives is only the beginning of an unfolding relationship in which there are continuously new discoveries and revelations of who he is. The more our knowledge of him grows, the more we will become partakers with him of the divine nature until his life is replicated in us. This was expressed by the apostle Paul in his letter to the infant churches in Galatia when he wrote, "My children, with whom I am again in labor until Christ *is formed* in you" (Galatians 4:19, emphasis mine).

The second stage in the maiden's relationship was that of increasing love. Through her many experiences with the king, she was coming to understand the process of transformation which was taking place in her life. To sum it up, she had entered a stage where she was learning a growing capacity for surrender.

This is evidenced by the king's articulating an appreciation for the beauty of her hair and of her neck, acknowledging her submission to his authority and the surrendering of her will to his. We also see in her the realization that she has become *his* private garden. More and more, the emphasis begins to shift away from her awareness of what he means to her to what she means to him.

Moving closer to the end of this second stage, we see an even deeper submission of her will to his. In chapter 5, verse 2, she says, "I was asleep, but my heart was awake. A voice, My beloved was knocking; 'Open to me, my sister, my darling, my dove, my perfect one.'"

At this time, although her outward person was asleep, her inner person was awake. For the Christian, this represents a deeper sensitivity to the activity of the Spirit within. This thought was captured by the apostle Paul when he testified, "I am crucified with Christ; and it is no longer I who live, but it is Christ who lives in me" (Galatians 2:20).

During this period, she also entered into fellowship with the one who endured the oil press of Gethsemane. Although she had known him in the heights, she was now beginning to know him in the depths. Her testimony was becoming that for which the apostle Paul earnestly longed when he wrote to the Philippians about his desire to "know him and the power of his resurrection and the fellowship of his sufferings, being conformed to his death; in order that I may attain to the resurrection from the dead" (Philippians 3:10–11).

What progress she has made! What advancement in her spiritual growth!

The bride emerges from this stage in brokenness and surrender. Like Jacob, who wrestled with God and became a prince, she has become a true princess.

Through an accumulation of all her experiences, she now sees her king not only as her lover, but as her friend. She can say, with confidence and a glad heart, "I am my beloved's, and my beloved is mine."

PART 3: MATURE LOVE

"I am my Beloved's, and His desire is for me."

SONG OF SONGS 7:10

Called By His Name

SONG OF SONGS, CHAPTER 6

"There are sixty queens and eighty concubines,
And maidens without number;
But my dove, my perfect one, is unique:
She is her mother's only daughter;
She is the pure child of the one who bore her
The maidens saw her and called her blessed,
The queens and the concubines also, and they praised her,
saying,
'Who is this that grows like the dawn,
As beautiful as the full moon,
As pure as the sun,
As awesome as an army with banners?'

"I went down to the orchard of nut trees
To see the blossoms of the valley,
To see whether the vine had budded
Or the pomegranates had bloomed.
Before I was aware, my soul set me
Over the chariots of my noble people."

"Come back, come back, O Shulammite;
Come back, come back, that we may gaze at you!"
"Why should you gaze at the Shulammite,
As at the dance of the two companies?"

SONG OF SONGS 6:8–13

As the days went by, I fell back into the rhythms of life with my husband, basking in his love. The king had secretly been busy planning an official gala to be held at the royal palace. He successfully kept it from me, but finally decided to let me in on his plan.

"I want to throw a party in your honor at the royal palace! It will be a lavish event for women only," he said one morning, with the joy of one who could contain a secret no longer.

At first, I was embarrassed and pleaded with him that it was not necessary, but it was no use. His exuberance could not be defeated. I reluctantly conceded and went along with his wishes. And of course, I soon grew excited about it as well.

It turned out that women from all over the kingdom had been invited to attend. The guest list included sixty queens, eighty concubines, and maidens without number. The party abounded with food, drink, and merrymaking.

As the women milled around talking and eating, suddenly the gentle music of the musicians was interrupted by trumpet blasts announcing the king's presence. All eyes focused on the balcony overlooking the hall. Finally, the king and I appeared. I stood close to his side with my arm draped over his. I was nervous. But at the same time, my heart burst with pride to be standing there with him. His face beamed with confidence as he relished the loud applause.

When the applause subsided, Solomon addressed the gathering. "Of all the women in my kingdom, this is my dove, my perfect one. There is no one like her on earth. There never has been, nor will there ever be. She is unique. She is her mother's only daughter, as pure and innocent as the day she was born. This is my Shulammite."

I watched as the women around the room gasped and gaped. I could hear their chatter. "He has even given her a new name—his *Shulammite*, the feminine form of his own name, Solomon! The two have truly become one! Could any woman be more blessed than she?"

The king raised his hands to quiet the growing buzz among the women. "I know that you all have questions about this love of mine. Who is she? Where did she come from? How did we meet? My darling, would you please share a short word with these ladies? I suggest you begin by telling them how we met."

I could feel myself tense, and for a moment my mouth went dry. I had never before spoken publicly—especially to such a large gathering—and there were so many eyes on me! I gazed around the room at the multitude of expectant faces. But he was there too—right beside me. Finally, the courage came to open my mouth.

"I am just a peasant princess," I said with a modest grin. "I come from a small village not far from Jerusalem. One beautiful morning, I went down to the grove of walnut trees and out to the valley to see the new spring growth. I wanted to see whether the grapevines had budded or the pomegranates were in bloom. Then, before I realized it, I found myself in the royal chariot with my beloved, and he whisked me away!"

What I said was brief, but it must have been enough. The women burst into spontaneous laughter! With that short anecdote, I seemed to have won their hearts.

The king joined in the laughter. Then he leaned over and whispered in my ear, "Do not be late!" With a gleam in his eyes, he gave me a quick smile and slipped away, releasing me to the crowd.

I made my way down the wide, winding steps to the palace floor. The women swarmed around me, pressing in and wanting to meet me. I slowly moved around the room, politely greeting and speaking with as many of the ladies as I could.

The queens and the concubines spoke among themselves, having nothing but praise for me. "Who is this that grows like the dawn? Her beauty only becomes more radiant the more we see her!" exclaimed one. "She is as beautiful as the full moon as she basks in the borrowed light of her sun, the king," chimed in another. "She is as pure as the sun," another added. "As awesome as an army with banners."

As the evening wore on, aware that the king was waiting for me, I began moving toward the door to make my exit. The maidens saw that I was attempting to leave the party and cried out, "Come back, come back, O Shulammite! Come back, come back, that we may gaze upon you!"

Ignoring their pleas, I turned to them and waved good-bye. I left the palace and hurried back to the king's residence.

POINTS TO CONSIDER

This is the first time the maiden-turned-queen is called "the Shulammite." Here we see the formal recognition of her oneness with the king.

Most Christians would readily admit that there is no feeling on this earth that can compare to the exhilaration of worshiping the Lord and being in his presence. But is there a still higher experience to be attained with the Divine?

Imagine holding a piece of clay in the palm of each hand. Could it be said that the lump of clay in the left hand is "in the presence of" the piece of clay in the right hand? Yes. Now, imagine moving your two hands closer together. Are the lumps of clay still in the presence of one another? Of course. Now, imagine bringing your hands within an inch of each other. They are still in one another's presence; they are closer than they have ever been. Is there any way they could possibly be closer to one another?

Yes! The two could become one.

In these passages in the Song, we see the queen called by Solomon's name. This shows her beginning to take on his character and nature. The two are becoming one.

Earlier in chapter 6, the king described his wife as being "as lovely as Jerusalem." This would suggest that she is taking on the heavenly characteristics of her eternal abode, the New Jerusalem (Revelation 21:1–2).

He also alleged that she was "as awesome as an army with banners." Banners speak of victory. When an army defeats its enemy, banners are raised in triumph. Spiritually, she had triumphed over her spiritual adversaries in heavenly realms, having overcome them through her union with the king.

Her beauty was compared to the full moon—not to a new moon or half-moon, but to a full moon—and she was said to be as pure as the sun. The sun is the source of all light and life. The moon only possesses a borrowed, reflected light. In spiritual terms, the sun spoken of here is not that fiery ball hanging in the sky, but rather, the sun within every believer: the Sun of Righteousness, Jesus Christ. The Shulammite is reflecting his fullness.

The glowing mass that lights our universe serves only as a picture of the real sun, Christ, for the day will come when it will no longer be needed. It will have served its purpose. In the New Jerusalem, Revelation 21:23 tells us, there will be "no need of the sun or of the moon to shine on it, for the glory of God has illumined it, and its lamp is the Lamb."

When believers turn within to face the Sun of Righteousness, they reflect his light.

In New Testament terms, the queen is one who, "with unveiled face, beholding as a mirror the glory of the Lord," is being transformed "into the same image from glory to glory, just as from the Lord, the Spirit" (2 Corinthians 3:18).

At this juncture, the Shulammite pictures for the believer one who has learned to abide in Christ and walk in the Spirit.

There is more to observe here. Nearly all of the descriptions of the king's love for his Shulammite focus on who she is, not on what she has done. They emphasize her character, not her deeds. Although deeds are of consequence, they are only the natural fruit of the woman she has come to be.

We see the same love emanating from the Father for the Son. Even before Jesus began his earthly ministry, when he came up out of the Jordan River after being baptized by John the Baptizer, the Father proclaimed from heaven, "You are My beloved Son, in You I am well-pleased" (Luke 3:22). The Scriptures leave no record of any previous miracles, profound teachings, acts of mercy, healings, or benevolent acts of kindness done by Jesus, although we can suppose that growing up his behavior was perfect—he was, all his life, the spotless Lamb of God. Be that as it may, for thirty years the record is silent on any significant acts that Jesus may have performed. Yet, he was the Father's delight—not based on a criterion of works, but because of his character. So it was with the Shulammite.

Shulammites are those who have learned to live by the divine life within them.
Shulammites are those whom the Book of Revelation would classify as *overcomers*.
Shulammites are what all "normal Christians" should be.

He who overcomes, I will make him a pillar in the temple of My God, and he will not go out from it anymore, and I will write on him the name of My God, and the name of the city of My God, the New Jerusalem, which comes down out of heaven from My God, and My new name. (Revelation 3:12)

THOUGHTS/PRAYERS

Thank you, Lord, that I am your Mrs.! I am your Shulammite. I don't ask you to make me your wife, because you have already done that. I am married to you in spirit. Our spirits are one. I just ask you to open my eyes as I turn my heart to you, and let me behold your glory. Make your impression on my soul. Shine on me, your Mrs., your mirror, so that I will walk in the light of your Spirit and your glory will be reflected in me.

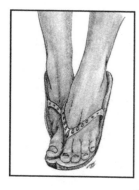

The Dance

SONG OF SONGS, CHAPTER 6

"Come back, come back, O Shulammite;
Come back, come back, that we may gaze at you!"

"Why should you gaze at the Shulammite,
As at the dance of the two companies?"

SONG OF SONGS 6:13

"How beautiful are your feet in sandals,
O prince's daughter!
The curves of your hips are like jewels,
The work of the hands of an artist.
Your navel is like a round goblet
Which never lacks mixed wine;
Your belly is like a heap of wheat
Fenced about with lilies.
Your two breasts are like two fawns,
Twins of a gazelle.
Your neck is like a tower of ivory,
Your eyes like the pools in Heshbon
By the gate of Bath-rabbim;
Your nose is like the tower of Lebanon,
Which faces toward Damascus.
Your head crowns you like Carmel,
And the flowing locks of your head are like purple threads;
The king is captivated by your tresses.

How beautiful and how delightful you are,
My love, with all your charms!
Your stature is like a palm tree,
And your breasts are like its clusters.
I said, 'I will climb the palm tree,
I will take hold of its fruit stalks.'
Oh, may your breasts be like clusters of the vine,
And the fragrance of your breath like apples,"

"And your mouth like the best wine!
It goes down smoothly for my beloved,
Flowing gently through the lips of those who fall asleep.
I am my beloved's,
And his desire is for me."

SONG OF SONGS 7:1–10

Leaving my beautiful queen at the party, I returned to my bedchamber, escorted by two of the palace guards. I bid them a good night and then entered my room.

At my request, two of my servants lit candles around the room and then prepared a warm bath for me. Dismissing them, I stepped into the bath and sank into its deep, soothing waters. I closed my eyes, laid my head back on the side of the aqua-colored pool, and enjoyed undisturbed relaxation. I smiled to myself as I remembered the words the women at the party had used to describe the queen.

Time seemed to evaporate. I may even have drifted into a light sleep. Finally, I emerged from the rejuvenating waters and dried myself off. I walked over to a long cedar table, upon which stood several bottles containing fragrant oils. Pouring a mixture of the oils into my hands and then rubbing them together, I ran my fingers through my hair and beard, coating them with the heady scent. I pulled back the curtains which surrounded my bed and slipped under the covers. Lounging against some of the large pillows, I looked around at the tall candles that dimly lit the room and watched the flickering light and patterns they created on the walls and ceiling. Then I lay back, sinking deeper into the pillows, and thought, *Surely, there is an aura in this room that is prime for love.*

Not long after, I heard her knock upon my door.

"It is me, my beloved," called the familiar voice.

"Enter, my dear; the door is open," I answered.

She pushed open the door and came inside. She looked lovely, clad in her beautiful gown and fine jewelry.

"I have been waiting for you to come," I said with a smile.

"It was difficult to get away," she replied. "There were so many guests!"

"From what I could tell, you made a brilliant appearance," I told her. Pride filled my voice.

"I think they liked me," she said, laughing softly. "As a matter of fact, as I was trying to leave, many of the women shouted to me, 'Come back, come back, O Shulammite; come back, come back, that we may gaze upon you! We want to see you dance—dance like the angels of God!'"

"What? They wanted to gaze upon you? They wanted you to dance?" I chuckled in amazement. "To gaze upon you is something reserved for my eyes only! This night I have been waiting to gaze upon you in ways which no other may do."

"You wish to gaze upon me?" she replied coyly as she slowly approached my bed and wrapped her arm around one of the ivory bedposts. The candlelight flickered on her hair. "And would you, also, like to see me dance?"

I responded at once. "As our father Jacob was met by two companies of angels at Mahanaim, let us surely engage one another. Let us dance!"

"I am ready to receive your advances." Her tone was light and teasing. "I am prepared to match your skills with mine. As you planned a lavish gala for me this night, I, in return, have planned a private gala for you. It is my gift. Let us indeed dance. Let us meet. Let us discover and enjoy what it is that comes from this engagement!"

With that, she began to slowly undress. Gracefully, she removed each article of jewelry and clothing until finally she stood naked before me at the foot of my bed, clad only in her sandals.

My heart pounded in my chest.

She stood there confidently, then flashed an inviting smile. Slowly, she began shuffling her feet. Closing her eyes, she began a slow-moving dance to a rhythm that could only be heard within her own head. Her hips followed, rocking gently to the same tempo.

My emotions spiraled upward. I rose hastily from my bed, dropping my feet to the floor. I began moving cautiously toward her, circling her, stalking her, waiting for the right moment to capture in my arms my willing prey.

Gazing at her feet, I said admiringly, "How beautiful are your feet in sandals, O prince's daughter!" Then I looked up into her face. Once again she smiled, imbibing with delight my compliment and advances.

My eyes returned to her feet and then began to scale her frame. "The curves of your hips are like jewels, the work of the hands of an artist. Tonight I will be that artist and lay hold of my masterpiece."

Next, I fixed on the ripples in her stomach that made patterns as she moved. "Your sleek navel is like a round goblet which never lacks mixed wine. In moments, I will drink from that wine." I breathed in as I moved even closer toward her. "Your belly is like a field of wheat that sways in the breeze."

Finally, I could restrain myself no longer. With one last step I reached for her as I fell to my knees. Wrapping my arms around her hips and waist, I began tenderly kissing her stomach, slowly sipping, as it were, her mixed wines with great delight.

She flung her head back and closed her eyes tightly. I felt her hands and her fingertips clasp the flesh of my shoulders in response to each loving display of affection.

She was enraptured. I was mesmerized.

Looking up, I gazed intensely at her gently swaying breasts. "I am inflamed with passion," I whispered in heavy breaths. "Your two breasts are firm. They are like two fawns, the twins of a gazelle. You have captured my body and my soul. They are yours to do with as you please."

She answered, "And, I am yours, my beloved. Fulfill every desire that you can imagine."

Rising to my feet, my body now glued to hers, my eyes moved to her slender neck and then to her eyes. "Your eyes are deep, my love, like the fish pools in Heshbon. Your nose is like the tower of Lebanon which faces toward Damascus."

At last, our lips came together, locking as one. Her lips were warm. I was enthralled with bliss as I enjoyed her long, soft kisses.

Gradually, I pulled back from her, and I raised my hands to clasp her cheeks. My eyes scoured every part of her face. "Your countenance crowns you like Carmel. The flowing locks that tumble upon your shoulders appear as purple threads in the candlelight, the color of royalty, meant only for a king."

Digging my fingers into her hair and intertwining them with her locks, I continued, "Your tresses have made me your captive. How beautiful and how delightful you are, my love, with all your charms!"

She pressed her breasts firmly into my chest and draped her arms around my neck. She stared intently into my eyes, as if pleading with me to talk no more.

"Your stature is tall, like the palm tree," I continued, in one last burst between kisses that grew more passionate, "and your breasts like its clusters. I will climb the palm tree. I will take hold of and caress its fruits."

With that, I quickly guided her down with me to the edge of the bed. Her sandals dropped off. We fell back against the soft pillows. She showered me with a thousand kisses as I did her. Our hands glided swiftly over each other's bodies, stopping only momentarily for intermittent grasps and caresses.

Then at last she sighed deeply—as did I—as we both reached the full height of love.

Gradually, our passion began to subside and our kisses turned softer. I could feel the short puffs of her breath against my face and mouth. "The fragrance of your breath is as crisp and sweet as apples, my love."

"Your tongue and your lips," she responded, "make me think of the best and rarest wine which goes down so smoothly. They flow gently through my lips as one who is falling asleep."

We lay together, exhausted, in the aftermath of pure ecstasy. I slid my arm gently under her neck and drew her body tightly to my own. She rested her head on my shoulder and nestled in the cradle of my arm. Looking up at me in the final moments before we were overtaken by sleep, she leaned over and tenderly whispered in my ear, "I have never before felt so secure in your love, my beloved husband. I am yours and will always be. And I know that your desire is for me!"

POINTS TO CONSIDER

This passage is probably one of the most erotic and sexually explicit portions in all of Scripture.

- Comparing different translations, it is clear that, because of the content, some interpreters had difficulties settling on an interpretation with which they were comfortable:
- "Come back, come back, O Shulammite; come back, come back, that we may gaze on you! Why would you gaze on the Shulammite as on the dance of Mahanaim?" (NIV)
- "Return, return, O Shulamite; return, return, that we may look upon thee. What will ye see in the Shulamite? As it were the company of two armies." (KJV)
- "Return, return to us, O maid of Shulam. Come back, come back, that we may see you again. Why do you stare at this young woman of Shulam, as she moves so gracefully between two lines of dancers?" (New Living Translation)
- "I began to flee, but they called to me Return, return, O Shulammite; return, return, that we may look upon you! [I replied] What is there for you to see in the [poor little] Shulammite? [And they answered] As upon a dance before two armies or a dance of Mahanaim." (Amplified)

- "Dance, dance, dear Shulammite, Angel-Princess! Dance, and we'll feast our eyes on your grace! Everyone wants to see the Shulammite dance her victory dances of love and peace." (*The Message*)

The "dance of the Mahanaim" is the literal translation, although many translators render the phrase as "the dance of two armies" or "the dance of two companies." *Mahanaim* literally means "two camps" or "two companies." It was the name Jacob gave to the place where he met God's angels in Genesis 32:1–2. Commentators believe he saw two companies of angels, possibly maneuvering, adjusting to one another as in a dance.

Erotic as this passage might be from a human perspective, the spiritual implications ought to forever revolutionize every believer's concept of God and his love. God is a *passionate God!* He desires intimacy! The playful, teasing, free, and intimate sexual relationship the Shulammite had with her husband ought to completely obliterate the notion that God is some stuffy, religious God who wants us to keep our distance, just obey him, and follow the rules. In this scene, as throughout the story, Solomon is a picture of Jesus Christ. The Shulammite is a picture of you and me—believers!

Although this passage is highly sensual, it is filled with significance for the believer who has reached this stage of spiritual maturity. In spiritual terms, this sumptuous description of the Shulammite depicts her as having become a strong marriage partner and co-worker, prepared to labor alongside her beloved in the fields of harvest. The first section of the description focuses on her readiness to reach the lost and minister to others, while the second section spotlights her strength.

Her feet were beautiful in sandals, which symbolizes her readiness to carry the gospel of peace.

How beautiful on the mountains are the feet of those who bring good news, who proclaim peace, who bring good tidings, who proclaim salvation, who say to Zion, "Your God reigns!" (Isaiah 52:7, also quoted in Romans 10:15)

. . . and having shod your feet with the preparation of the gospel of peace. (Ephesians 6:15)

The curves of her hips were like jewels, the work of the hands of an artist. The way she walked (that is, the way in which she conveys Christ's message) was in itself a work of art and attractive to others.

Her navel was like a round goblet which never lacked mixed wine; her mouth was like the best wine—she had a reservoir of joy within which flowed from her lips and was a continual supply to others.

Her belly was a heap of wheat. She was full of desire to take part in the wheat harvest, the spiritual ingathering of souls.

Her eyes were like the fish pools of Heshbon by the gate of Bath-rabbim. Solomon saw in her eyes the longing to cast her nets and bring in a catch of fish. She had become, like Peter, a fisher of men, and her influence would be great. (*Bath-rabbim* means "daughter of many.")

Her nose was like the tower of Lebanon: she had a strong sense of smell, representing her spiritual discernment, by which she was able to discern what was happening in the unseen.

Her head was crowned like Carmel, the place where the Lord demonstrated his power through Elijah.

Her stature was like the palm tree. Palm trees are tall and strong. They have deep roots. They hold their ground even in strapping winds, and they bear fruit even in dry places.

Her breasts were like a cluster of dates or clusters of grapes from the vine. She was equipped to impart sweetness and joy into the lives of others.

The fragrance of her breath was like apples—fresh and crisp. She communicated the gospel with freshness and newness.

In this scene, we see a husband and wife totally free with one another; completely uninhibited and able to enjoy to the fullest all that each has to offer the other. This is oneness. This can only be achieved as the woman feels the security and confidence that comes with knowing that "I am my beloved's, and his desire is toward me."

THOUGHTS/PRAYERS

Lord Jesus, as I try to conceive of the idea that you love me in as passionate and consuming a way as is described in this love relationship between Solomon and his bride, it is beyond my comprehension. Many false concepts of you in my mind get in the way of believing that you really feel this strongly about me. Lord, obliterate those false, religious, man-made concepts. I want to be able to give you what you desire. I want my love for you to be as free and as uninhibited as the Shulammite's love for her king. I want to be able to dance before you and excite you! Lord, draw me. I want to experience the fullness of my oneness with you. Bring me to a place where I can receive this kind of love from you. Make me to know, beyond a doubt, that I am yours and your desire is for me!

"As we approach the marriage song, the Song of the Bridegroom and the Bride, to read and to weigh your work, we call upon you, O Spirit of holiness. We want you to fill us with your love, O Love, so that we may understand love's song—so that we, too, may be made in some degree participants in the dialogue of the holy Bridegroom and the Bride, and so that what we read about may come to pass within us.

"For this reason, the Holy Spirit, in handing over to human creatures the song of spiritual love, attires the whole of its interior, spiritual, and divine subject matter in the external garment provided by the images of fleshly love—and this precisely in order that, because love alone can fully grasp the things of God, fleshly love is being introduced to spiritual love and passing over into it, may quickly lay hold of what it is like."

WILLIAM OF SAINT THIERRY, TWELFTH CENTURY

A Woman for the World

SONG OF SONGS, CHAPTER 7

"Come, my beloved, let us go out into the country,
Let us spend the night in the villages.
Let us rise early and go to the vineyards;
Let us see whether the vine has budded
And its blossoms have opened,
And whether the pomegranates have bloomed.
There I will give you my love."

"The mandrakes have given forth fragrance;
And over our doors are all choice fruits,
Both new and old,
Which I have saved up for you, my beloved."

SONG OF SONGS 7:11–13

The following morning, the king and I shared breakfast together on our balcony overlooking the city. Still basking in the warmth of our love from the previous evening, Solomon said to me, "Last night was astonishing, my darling. Beyond words. We will perhaps rarely know such a love as we have known before this dawning."

I reached over and placed my hand on his arm. "You are right, my beloved," I said. "Last night I felt so alive, so free. I have never before felt so uninhibited. It was as though, in giving to you, I had become the greatest recipient of love that could ever be imagined. I could never have dreamed or imagined that two people could share such oneness, such intimacy."

"We must have touched what the father and mother of our race first experienced in the garden," said the king, "when the first humans loved one another in their innocence and were totally unashamed."

We both smiled as we savored the memory of the night before.

It was Solomon who finally broke the silence. "I have something to discuss with you, my dear. I noticed something while watching you a few days ago. I have not had the time to talk with you about it until now. Tell me if I am wrong: when I saw you gazing out the window the other night, I perceived a distant look in your eyes. It was as if you were thinking of someone far away. Was it, perhaps, that you were thinking of your mother and your brothers whom you left behind in the village?"

"You are very perceptive, my king," I replied. "The answer is both yes and no. I have thought some about them. But I have been so occupied with you here in Jerusalem and traveling on all the expeditions you plan that I have rarely had the time to let my thoughts dwell upon them. However, this one thing I *do* think about a great deal: I see the poor people who come daily into the city with their carts, wagons, and meager belongings, and I think of their kind often. They represent my roots and the place from which I come." Pointing to the crowded, narrow streets, I said, "Look down there and see for yourself what I mean."

Peering down from our balcony, Solomon gazed intently at the slow-moving swarm of humanity winding its way through the streets of Jerusalem. "Hearing you speak," mused the king, "reminds me of the exhortation my mother gave to you on our wedding day when she said, 'The excellent wife extends her hand to the poor and stretches out her hands to the needy.'"

"And, to you, my king, she said, 'Open your mouth for the mute, for the rights of all the unfortunate. Open your mouth, judge righteously, and defend the rights of the afflicted and needy.'"

"I know of your concern for the underprivileged, my dear," Solomon answered. "Do you remember last night during our dance, when I told you that your eyes were like the fish pools of Heshbon? I have seen in your eyes a concern for the poor and the needy in the kingdom—for people who have come from humble beginnings, like yourself. I know that you would like to see the benefits of the realm in which we live fall upon them as well. And, like a good fisherman, I know that you would like to cast your nets and bring a great catch of people into the wealth of this kingdom. What better confidante could I, as king, have? You know the struggles and the hardships the poor and downtrodden face. I am open to your counsel."

Then his eyes lit up. "I know!" he said. "Tomorrow let us go out into the country and spend the night in the villages. You can show me what your eyes see."

"That would be wonderful!" I exclaimed. "As privileged as we are to drink from cups of gold at every meal, it is not the way most people live. We shall go to the villages. We shall talk with the people. And we shall see how some of the vast wealth of this kingdom in which we live can be shared to bring them joy and hope."

"Excellent!" Solomon declared. He folded his napkin and placed it on his plate. "Let us rise early and go also to the vineyards. Let us see whether the vine has budded and the blossoms have opened, and whether the pomegranates have blossomed. Then we will go to the villages and spend the night. If I can give you my love in the palace upon a bed of ivory, can I not also give it to you in the villages on a mat of straw? It is all ours to experience together, my love."

"Your offer is irresistible!" I said. "We can eat of the mandrake roots and draw from their love powers. We shall open wide the doors of our hearts to one another once again. We will delight in not only the choicest, familiar fruits, but you shall taste of things new as well, which I have saved for you, my beloved! Only promise me one thing."

"Anything you ask, my love."

"Only promise me that you will not forget the poor," I said, jokingly, as I smiled and touched my finger to his nose.

POINTS TO CONSIDER

The king and his wife set off on an amorous adventure to the countryside and the villages. There, once again, they planned a rendezvous with love.

Mandrake roots were thought to have love powers and were frequently used to promote fertility. *Mandrake* in Hebrew means "love plant."

At this stage in the Song, the king's wife and lover has become his co-laborer.

Jesus told his disciples that, "The harvest is plentiful, but the laborers are few; therefore beseech the Lord of the harvest to send out laborers into His harvest" (Luke 10:2). The Shulammite now represents one of those co-laborers. She is one of the few. She is one set apart for service.

Like Moses, who paid the price by spending forty years in the wilderness in preparation to lead God's people to the Promised Land; like David, who was anointed as a young lad but waited for years, dodging spears and hiding in holes in the mountains as part of his apprenticeship to become king; this Shulammite was now fully prepared to go with the king to the country, the villages, and the vineyards, and to know his love there. For the Christian, this portion of the Song represents being set apart to serve and being sent out into the fields of harvest.

There are different levels from which to appreciate the Shulammite's readiness for service. The first is to see her as one who models for all Christians, at any stage of spiritual maturity, the capacity to serve. Such a one must also be willing to go through a time of preparation first.

Before being sent out throughout the Roman Empire with the gospel, the apostle Paul had his own "secret dealings" with God. Paul was called while on the road to Damascus, but he was not sent out by the Holy Spirit for another twelve to fourteen years. (The sending occurred at a prayer meeting in Antioch that changed history, when he and Barnabas received their commission in Acts 13:2: "While they were ministering to the Lord and fasting, the Holy Spirit said, "Set apart for Me Barnabas and Saul for the work to which I have called them.") There was his time in the Arabian Desert after his conversion and his time in Tarsus, where we know little about what he was doing. This all took place before he was asked by Barnabas to serve alongside him in the church at Antioch. There, God used Paul to speak and teach from house to house—but this was still but preparation for an even greater work, that of taking the gospel to the entire Gentile world.

If God should send you and commission you for service, don't be surprised if he sends you somewhere you would never choose to go. Paul had been trained as a Pharisee. He was from the tribe of Benjamin, a Hebrew of Hebrews, steeped in all the knowledge and background of Hebrew culture. He was educated by the finest scholars in all of Israel—yet God sent him to the Gentiles!

Imagine Paul trying to impress some illiterate Scythian slave with his pedigree, or with his knowledge of Jewish laws and dietary customs. Imagine him using some example from the Torah from the life of Moses, and his audience reacting, "Moses who?" Good Jews were not even supposed to have dealings with the Gentiles! Yet this was the mission field to which God sent Paul.

Have you found your "mission field," the area where God has called you to serve? Have you found your village; your vineyard?

Yours could be a work with hospice, the handicapped, or the homeless. Possibly, God has placed you among politicians or the poor. Maybe, through some seeming quirk, accident, or even tragedy, you have come in contact with a circle of people with whom you would never have chosen to be, but among them you now have a platform.

One way to determine where that field of service for you might be, whether it is one lost soul, one solitary saint, or the multitudes, is to look at where "life's leading" is taking you.

Where God leads, there is the sense of life and peace.

For the mind set on the Spirit is life and peace. (Romans 8:6)

For all who are being led by the Spirit of God, these are the sons of God. (Romans 8:14)

In the Song, the king says to his willing companion, "Let us see whether the vine has budded and its blossoms have opened, and whether the pomegranates have bloomed."

Budding and blooming are evidences of life. Even if what you are doing or who you are doing it with—whatever constitutes your village—goes unnoticed by the crowds, if that is where you find the Lord's presence and a sense of life, then invest yourself! That is the place where he wants to show you his love.

But there is also a second level from which the Shulammite's stature can be appreciated.

Look around and think of people you know who have been given some type of ministry. Most of these servants of God are laboring in their own vineyards. But is there another level of service present here? Look again. Do you see those who have outgrown their own personal ministries and are now *also* laboring in the vineyards of others?

These are God's generals. These are the ones who see beyond building their own ministries and their own empires. They are concerned about the kingdom. Their sphere of work may be whole cities, regions, or nations. They are the ones who move in and out of different vineyards because they have too much spiritual capacity to be confined to any one group or people.

This is who Solomon's life companion had become.

Look at the plurals in the wording he uses: "Come, my beloved, let us go out into the country, let us spend the night in the villages [plural], let us rise early and go to the vineyards [plural]."

This woman had become a woman for the world.

When the Lord looks at you, does he see in your eyes the fish pools of Heshbon? Is there a burden in your heart for the lost of this world? Would you become like this lady? The Lord would have legions like her. But why are there so few? What is he waiting for? Luke 10:2 tells us, "The harvest is plentiful, but the laborers are few; therefore beseech the Lord of the harvest to send out laborers into His harvest."

The Lord is looking for volunteers who are ready to join him, to go where he goes and to do what he wants to do. He is waiting to send out those who are willing to be sent and to go through the preparation. Is there anything preventing you from becoming one of those few?

Lord, take me to the villages where you want to take me. But prepare me first, so that I will be able to work with you in the harvest. Wherever that may be, I want you to show me your love there. Teach me to follow that sense of life and peace within me. The fields are white; the laborers are few. Lord, make me like this Shulammite. Make me one of your co-laborers.

The Inward Instructor

SONG OF SONGS, CHAPTER 8

"Oh that you were like a brother to me
Who nursed at my mother's breasts.
If I found you outdoors, I would kiss you;
No one would despise me, either.
I would lead you and bring you
Into the house of my mother, who used to instruct me;
I would give you spiced wine to drink from the juice of my pomegranates.
Let his left hand be under my head
And his right hand embrace me."

"I want you to swear, O daughters of Jerusalem,
Do not arouse or awaken my love
Until she pleases."

SONG OF SONGS 8:1–4

Late one morning, after we had returned from an unforgettable trip to the villages, the king summoned me to his throne room. I entered and stood before him at the bottom of the six steps leading to the throne, adorned on each side by twelve magnificent, golden lions, the likes of which were seen nowhere else in any kingdom of this world. The throne itself was like none other. It was made of ivory, overlaid with gold, and studded with the most spectacular rubies, sapphires, emeralds, and other precious stones, all sparkling in their brilliance.

The king spoke to me and informed me that he intended to go on a tour of Jerusalem that afternoon. The announcement came as no surprise to me, for he frequently toured the city. But his purpose for summoning me was to invite me to go

His Desire Is for Me 〜 171

with him. I agreed, and I went back to my room to prepare.

We left the palace later that afternoon, surrounded by an escort of armed guards, and made our way through the upper city, passing expensive homes and spacious gardens until we came to the lower city with its narrow streets, marketplaces, shops, and bazaars. Our eyes took in all the chaos. Here, the peace within the palace walls was replaced by the banter of man and animal, and by the fragrances of incense, flowers, and exotic spices, with a blend of smells coming from cooking pots and the stench from debris that lined the streets.

As we strolled along, we passed a rather small, vacant property between two shops. On it, several dozen children had gathered to play. We stopped to watch.

Approaching the area where the children were playing was a young boy with his twin sister. They were holding hands. The young girl saw some of her friends, so she gave her brother a quick kiss on the cheek, then ran to join them.

Seeing this provoked me to turn to the king and ask, "How is it that in our culture, we find no problem when young children display their affections in public? We actually find their innocence to be adorable—they hold hands or kiss one another without giving the slightest thought as to what others may think. At what age do we become too old for that? When do we grow so old that we must hide our true feelings for the ones we love and not exhibit them openly?"

The king blinked.

"Well, my darling," he slowly replied, "I cannot cite a specific age, but at some point it just becomes inappropriate to express love for another in the public arena."

"Do you think that is the way it *should* be?" I answered. "What about you and me? How would you feel if I were to kiss you in public?"

He looked a bit flustered as he spread his hands and said, "My love, I would welcome your kisses at any time. But it would be in opposition to all of our customs and traditions. It is just not something that is done—especially if it is the woman who initiates the kiss."

The children were still laughing and playing, and I followed them with my eyes as I responded, "Oh, that you were like a brother to me, just like these two children here on the street. If I found you outdoors, I would kiss you, and no one would despise me."

The king laughed. His handsome smile made me smile in return.

"That would be a first," he said, as he continued to chuckle, "especially for the *king* to receive a kiss in public!"

"My mother used to instruct me about what is proper and what is not," I said. "But now you are my instructor, O king. I would let your instruction overrule that

His Desire Is for Me ∽ 172

of my mother. In fact, if given the opportunity, I would lead you and bring you into her very house and mix you spiced wine to drink from the juice of my pomegranates. Even there, I would not hide nor withhold my affections for you, if that is what you would want. All that matters to me now is what *you* think, my beloved."

The king took me by the arm, and we turned to go back into the heart of the city. I looked up at Solomon and gazed into his eyes. Without words, he seemed to be telling me, *This is the kind of love I wish from you—your wholehearted trust and abandoned desire, without a care for what others might think. This is the kind of love I wish from you most of all.*

We returned to the palace. The king escorted me down the long corridor to my chamber. I took his sleeve before he could leave me. My desire for him had been building all afternoon. "Come into my chamber, my beloved," I said, "and lie down with me. I yearn for your left hand to be under my head and your right hand to embrace me once again."

Gladly complying with my request, Solomon entered my chamber and closed the door.

I poured some water from a pitcher into a large bowl. Then we both began to disrobe. We took turns dipping our hands into the bowl and splashing water on our bodies to freshen up. Next, I opened a vial of sweet-smelling perfume, and with my fingers, placed it behind my ears and alongside my neck. Then we slipped under the covers on the bed and made love.

When it was time for him to leave, I accompanied him to the door.

"I like to see your long, black hair hanging down like that," Solomon said as he leaned against the wall beside the door and ran his fingers through my hair. "Slightly unkempt, falling sensuously on your shoulders. Your eyes have a starry glaze upon them, an indication perhaps, that our amorous time together was pleasurable?"

I giggled slightly at his teasing. The king lingered at my door as we exchanged parting words.

Then, suddenly, from one end of the corridor, we heard women's voices and the pattering of sandals upon the stone hallway. It was about a dozen of the daughters of Jerusalem. Shocked to find the king and me standing there alone together, they came to an abrupt halt.

Seeing the women, I instantly turned to the king. I reached up, draped my arms around his neck, and planted a long, deep, passionate kiss upon his lips. Then, turning around, I withdrew into my room and closed the door.

My heart was beating with exhilaration as I shut myself into the room. I could only imagine how this unexpected, spontaneous display of public affection had left the king momentarily without composure. Later, he confessed to me that it gave him inexplicable joy!

I listened from behind my door as he walked briskly down the corridor, straight toward the gawking women. As he stopped in front of them, I heard him admonish them in a loud, stern voice, "Why do you stare? Is it so unusual for the king and his wife to show their affections? Do not disturb my love. I want you *to swear*, O daughters of Jerusalem, that you will not arouse or awaken her until she pleases."

POINTS TO CONSIDER

In the beginning of her quest for intimacy with the king, the maiden asked for his kisses: "May he kiss me with the kisses of his mouth." Now, she is the one initiating the kiss. Before, she expressed her affection for him only in private, but now she has no inhibitions about expressing it, even in public.

"I would lead you and bring you into the house of my mother, who used to instruct me," she says in verse 2. The "house of my mother" represents the church. For today's Shulammite to express these thoughts would be to say, "Lord, you have been so rich to me. My ardent yearning is to bring what I have known of you back to the church so that they may know you as I have."

It was also the church that "used to" instruct her. Now, it is the king alone. He is her instructor. He is her authority.

It may sound strange or even frightening to some that Christ alone could be your authority. Aren't we told in the Scriptures to "Obey your leaders and submit to them, for they keep watch over your souls as those who will give account" (Hebrews 13:17)?

The importance of the church is not to be diminished, for the church is the Lord's body; nor is what you can learn from others in the body of Christ to be disdained; but there should come a time in the life of every believer when Christ becomes real enough to you that *He alone* becomes your tutor.

> As for you, the anointing which you received from Him abides in you, and you have no need for anyone to teach you; but as His anointing teaches you about all things, and is true and is not a lie, just as it has taught you, you abide in Him. (1 John 2:27)

Nowhere in the Scriptures are we told to mindlessly obey our leaders. The word translated "obey" in the Hebrews 13 text actually means "let yourself be persuaded by." The word for "submit" is not an order, but rather, it means "to yield." What this verse actually says is, "Allow yourselves to be persuaded by your leaders (because of their example, their godly character, their servant natures, their familiarity with God's ways and his truth) and be willing to yield to them."

Both the words for "obey" and "submit" indicate that there is a choice involved. Never are we admonished to obey another Christian out of fear or duty, as a soldier compelled to obey the command of a superior.

Nowhere does the Scripture teach that one believer has "authority over" another believer. That place is reserved for Christ alone. In God's kingdom, God is king.

To make sure we don't miss this point, the Holy Spirit tells us in 1 John 4:1, "Beloved, do not believe every spirit, but test the spirits to see whether they are from God, because many false prophets have gone out into the world." We should always inquire of God as to the things we are taught, to determine if they are of him.

In the Old Testament, the people of Israel told Samuel that they wanted a king to rule over them like the other nations. This was a foolish request. When Samuel inquired of God about it, the answer he received was, "Listen to the voice of the people in all they say to you, for they have not rejected you, but they have rejected Me from being their king" (1 Samuel 8:7).

Because we are children of God, we are in God's kingdom and have direct access to our king. There are no intermediaries. Access to authority is not several people removed, but is within us. This is rather strange in comparison to earthly kingdoms!

Nevertheless, it is there, deep within our spirits, where God, the Father of Spirits, sits enthroned and instructs us.

Furthermore, we had earthly fathers to discipline us, and we respected them; shall we not much rather be subject to the *Father of spirits,* and live? For they disciplined us for a short time as seemed best to them, but He disciplines us for our good, so that we may share His holiness. All discipline for the moment seems not to be joyful, but sorrowful; *yet to those who have been trained by it,* afterwards it yields the peaceful fruit of righteousness." (Hebrews 12:9–11, emphasis mine)

This is the covenant that the Lord has made with us. These were his wedding vows:

I will put My laws into [your mind], and I will write them on [your heart], and I will be [your] God, and [you] shall be My people. And they shall not teach everyone his fellow citizen, and everyone his brother, saying, "Know

the Lord." For all will know Me [including you!], from the least to the greatest of them. (Hebrews 9:10–11)

There will be times of trouble and confusion when we will need to fellowship
with others in order to find the Lord's will and understand what he is saying to us.
After all, we are part of his body, and one way God speaks to us is through other
members of the body. In those difficult times, we must learn to lean on the lilies (see
summary of Section 1). But in our daily walk with the Lord, we must learn to trust
our inward instructor.

Finally, in this passage, we catch a glimpse of the mystery of all mysteries.

First, we see Solomon, the king, of whom it says in 1 Kings 10:18–20 that he
"made a great throne of ivory [representing the great white throne upon which God
sits] and overlaid it with refined gold. There were six steps to the throne and a round
top to the throne at its rear, and arms on each side of the seat, and two lions standing beside the arms. Twelve lions were standing there on the six steps on the one side
and on the other; nothing like it was made for any other kingdom."

This throne upon which Solomon sat was magnificent, yet ominous. The twelve
lions lining the steps on either side were breathtaking, yet dreadful. Few men dared
even to approach the king, but those who did fell on their faces before him in absolute
fear.

In contrast to the king and his throne, we see the maiden, who has become his
Shulammite. She has become bone of his bone, flesh of his flesh, spirit of his spirit.
This is the one who could enter the king's presence, yes, even the throne room itself,
without hesitation and without fear.

Here is the great paradox: He who is beyond all description in brightness and
holiness, purity and innocence, ruling over all space and time and all nations past,
present, and future, is also in love with a woman. That woman is his church, but that
woman is also you! His love is a passionate love, yet a simple love. It is a beautiful love,
and it is a perfect love. Finally, it is an approachable love.

Such is the picture captured here in the relationship between the Shulammite
and her king. What an incredible God we have!

THOUGHTS/PRAYERS

Meditate on this thought for a moment: How comfortable have you become
expressing your love for the Lord in public? Do those around you cause you to hold
back? Why? Maybe the Lord would have you pray through those fears.

The most important thing is to realize that God, in Christ, through the Holy

Spirit, dwells within you. And he *is* love. He is the Father of spirits who is in *your spirit,* teaching you, disciplining you—and yes, loving you—with a view that you will share in his holiness and righteousness.

Quiet your soul and listen for his still, small voice. Learn to follow that sense of life and peace and be trained by the tutor within. The anointing within you is reliable and practical. Learn to trust him. He is your king, and he is your God.

Lord Jesus, thank you that you live inside of me. Thank you that I can approach you without hesitation or fear. Thank you that you want to be my teacher. Train me to walk in your ways, to hear your voice, and to pay attention to your anointing within. Be my tutor, my instructor, and my lover!

Do Not Be Disturbed

SONG OF SONGS, CHAPTER 8

"I want you to swear, O daughters of Jerusalem,
Do not arouse or awaken my love until she pleases."

SONG OF SONGS 8:4

It was another extraordinarily beautiful day to visit the garden. I dressed in clothes in which I could work. The queen dressed casually in a long, camel-colored, flowing gown. She sat, relaxed, on one of the benches that decorated the landscape, enjoying the peace and tranquility. Leaning her head back on its wooden frame, she closed her eyes, faced the sun, and drank in the warmth of its rays.

I was only a few feet away on my hands and knees in one of the spice beds, working in the fertile soil. One by one I plucked from the ground the small heads of weeds that had broken through the earth and were attempting to lay claim to the space reserved for my favorite spices.

Suddenly, the silence was broken as the queen erupted behind me in a spontaneous burst of laughter. I turned to watch as she continued to giggle, until finally her laughter subsided.

"You must share with me your source of your amusement," I demanded, exhibiting a smile of my own.

"I was just recalling," she said, "a recent occurrence that I found to be quite entertaining."

"And what was that?" I inquired.

"Do you remember that day outside my bedchamber, in the hallway, when you confronted the daughters of Jerusalem and made them swear not to awaken me?"

"Yes," I replied.

"Well, I was listening from behind my door. You must have been somewhat embarrassed, but I applaud how you came to my defense, even though I thought it to be quite funny. You were my true champion!"

I reclined in the dirt, propping myself up with my elbows. Then I gazed up at her.

"Yes, I remember. But that was not the first time they received such an admonition," I mused. "The earliest occasion was at evening's end, the first time you accompanied me to the banqueting hall at the winter palace. I could see in your eyes then that you were smitten by love. I was determined to protect that sacred power as it laid claim to your being and coursed through your emotions. I wanted you to savor that intoxicating feeling, like an aged wine upon your palette, until the moment your eyelids finally closed for the night—yes, even until the morning, when you would awaken to meet such thoughts once again. That is why I had to caution the daughters of Jerusalem not to arouse you until you pleased. Although their intentions are mostly good, at times they can be meddlesome."

"You are wise, my king. You allowed love to smolder in my heart that night and through the next morning, and it has done nothing but continue to burn ever since."

"I am not finished," I said. "I am reminded of yet a third time in which they received the same admonition from my lips. It was the night you sought me in the streets of Jerusalem. When you found me, you clung to me."

Her face sobered as she thought back. "Yes, at that time too, my thoughts were desperately consumed with love. I understood that all of the wonderful benefits you had bestowed upon me could not compare with the simple but exalted pleasure of just being with you. It was not the gifts, but the giver whom I desired. To rest and to delight and to meditate on your love was just what my heart needed."

"It is in such moments that love needs to be protected most of all," I replied. "For when love takes root in the heart, it requires time and nurture, without distraction, to grow and to blossom."

Rolling over, I again searched the fertile soil for another unwanted weed. Spotting one, I reached out and gently tugged on the small, seemingly innocent stalk until it broke free from the ground. Lifting it up for us both to see, I inspected it, then tossed it into the reed basket beside me along with all the other weeds.

"I cannot permit these sinister invaders to suck the nutrients out of this productive soil. They disturb the roots and stifle the growth of these precious spices, which I have planted for my own enjoyment," I said. "In the same way, I must also keep a watchful eye on the daughters of Jerusalem lest they upset what is growing in the precious soil of your heart."

"Do I perceive anger in your voice?" the queen asked, in a teasing tone.

"A little," I said.

"Are you comparing the daughters of Jerusalem to weeds, my lord?"

"I know they do their best to honor me and that they love serving in the palace. But sometimes, they place their love for service and following the rules above my interests. They do not understand, as you do, my own deep longing for love. When they reason that it is time for you to awaken, they do not perceive that to love me would mean allowing you to lie on your bed and think about love or plan some creative way in which to express that love to me. When I recognize that their actions might hinder love, then I must step in."

I paused for a moment, looking away from the garden, with its weeds and its spices, to my wife.

"At such times, they are indeed like these weeds and must be thwarted. For have I not told you before that you are my beautiful garden of spices?"

The queen sat quietly on the bench with her hands folded in her lap, looking into my face. Finally, she broke her silence.

"I adore you, my king. Nothing gives me greater joy than just being with you."

"And nothing gives me more joy," I said, "than to see you suck all the nutrients from the rich soil of my love, to drink from the stream of my provision, and to bathe in the warmth of my protection. Seeing you receive all that I have to give you is, indeed, my greatest joy. Service, as these others give me, has never been what I require of you. The greatest gift you could ever give to me is simply your freewill offering of love."

POINTS TO CONSIDER

Three times in the Song of Songs, the king admonishes the daughters of Jerusalem not to arouse nor awaken his love until she pleases. The third time, he makes them *swear* not to arouse or awaken her.

Each time this happens, she is in a place of thinking intimately and lovingly about her beloved:

- "Let his left hand be under my head and his right hand embrace me." (Song of Songs 2:6)
- "I found him whom my soul loves; I held on to him and would not let him go until I had brought him to my mother's house, and into the room of her who conceived me." (Song of Songs 3:4)
- "I would lead you and bring you into the house of my mother who used to instruct me; I would give you spiced wine to drink from the juice of my pomegranates. Let his left hand be under my head and his right hand embrace me." (Song of Songs 8:2–3)

At each stage, from the time of her initial love, through her phase of increasing love, and all the way to her maturity, the daughters of Jerusalem are warned repeatedly by the king to stay away, to not interrupt nor disturb the maiden from her rest and from expressing her intimate desires for him.

Who are these daughters?

These were other maidens who knew of the king but only from afar, who had not run after him and advanced in spiritual maturity as she had.

These daughters represent other believers in Christ who, because of their superficial knowledge of him, often try to upset those who truly love him and are pursuing him as their all.

Most often, these followers of Christ are still living under the Law or a set of Christian laws they have taken upon themselves and are seeking to impose on others. They are the rigid, the legalists, and those who would try to pull back the seeking ones so the seekers will look more like themselves. They are the Marthas, the Pharisees, and sometimes even the disciples.

Now as they were traveling along, He entered a village; and a woman named Martha welcomed Him into her home. She had a sister called Mary, who was seated at the Lord's feet, listening to His word. But Martha was distracted with all her preparations; and she came up to Him and said, "Lord, do you not care that my sister has left me to do all the serving alone? Then tell her to help me."

But the Lord answered and said to her, "Martha, Martha, you are worried and bothered about so many things; but *only one thing* is necessary, for Mary has chosen the good part, which shall not be taken away from her. (Luke 10: 38–42, emphasis mine)

Martha was distracted, and she wanted to draw Mary away from the only thing that was necessary. If Martha had gotten her way, Mary would have been distracted too!

Martha attempted to serve the Lord. Mary let the Lord serve her. Martha tried to feed him. Mary fed on his words. Martha was out in the kitchen. Mary sat at his feet. Martha was bothered and caught up in her work. Mary was at peace and rest. Martha was talking. Mary was listening. Martha wanted someone else to help her. Mary was being helped by the Lord. Martha tried to give. Mary had learned to receive.

Sometimes, it is necessary to stop and ask ourselves, are we serving the Lord, or is Jesus serving us? Are we working for the Lord, or are we allowing the Lord to work in and through us? In all these ways in which Martha and Mary are compared, with whom do we identify? What changes need to be made?

In our pursuit of Christ, assaults on that pursuit can come from many quarters. They may come from a friend, a relative, a parent. They may come in the form of seemingly innocent comments like, "Why do you spend so much time with the Lord?" "You should be doing this or that." "Why aren't you doing more?" "You have a lot to give. Why don't you start something?" "Why aren't you more involved in your church, in giving, in Bible studies, in missions?" "You should be under some spiritual authority." You should, you should, you should…

The question is, do we heed these voices, or do we focus on "the one thing" our Lord says is important?

Where have we succumbed to the demands of those who want to distract us and draw us away from sitting at the Lord's feet and resting in him, into some counterfeit, eternally worthless "religious" service? It may be time to set some boundaries.

Again, we see an attempt to thwart one with an intense devotion to Christ from her worship at the house of Simon the Pharisee:

And there was a woman in the city who was a sinner; and when she learned that He was reclining at the table in the Pharisee's house, she brought an alabaster vial of perfume, and standing behind him at His feet, weeping, she began to wet His feet with her tears, and kept wiping them with the hair of her head, and kissing His feet and anointing them with the perfume. Now when the Pharisee who had invited Him saw this, he said to himself, "If this man were a prophet He would know who and what sort of person this woman is who is touching Him, that she is a sinner." (Luke 7:37–39)

Next it says, "And Jesus answered him…"

Simon was only *thinking* this thought to himself. The words never came out of his mouth. But Jesus discerned what he was thinking and answered him, making a lesson of the one who would rob Jesus of such an act of abandoned, unbridled devotion.

And Jesus answered him, "Do you see this woman? I entered your house; you gave me no water for My feet, but she has wet My feet with her tears and wiped them with her hair. You gave Me no kiss; but she, since the time

I came in, has not ceased to kiss my feet. You did not anoint My head with oil, but she anointed My feet with perfume. For this reason I say to you, her sins, which are many, have been forgiven, for she loved much; but he who is forgiven little, loves little." (Luke 7:44–47)

"I adjure you… that you do not arouse or awaken my love until she pleases."

At Bethany, we even see the disciples themselves attempting to interrupt love in the house of Simon the leper:

Now when Jesus was in Bethany, at the home of Simon the leper, a woman came to Him with an alabaster vial of very costly perfume, and she poured it on His head as He reclined at the table. But the disciples were indignant when they saw this, and said, "Why this waste? For this perfume might have been sold for a high price and the money given to the poor."

But Jesus, aware of this, said to them, "Why do you bother the woman? For she has done a good deed to Me. For you always have the poor with you; but you do not always have Me. For when she poured this perfume on My body, she did it to prepare Me for burial. Truly I say to you, wherever this gospel is preached in the whole world, what this woman has done will also be spoken of in memory of her." (Matthew 26:6–13)

Would you like for the Lord to memorialize you? Would you like what you have done to be spoken of wherever the gospel is preached? Would you, like Mary, be one of those elite to be inducted into Lord's Hall of Fame? If so, what are the qualifications?

Is it how much you have given to help the poor, or is it how much of your life you have given to him? Is it claiming to be his follower—yet never really taking him at his word, especially at times when it may not really seem to make sense—or, like Mary, heeding his word and making him your treasure?

Jesus had just finished telling the disciples that after two days, the Passover was coming and the Son of Man would be handed over for crucifixion (Matthew 26:2). All of the disciples were in the house of Simon the leper that day and heard what Jesus said, but it was only Mary who believed and responded to his words. Knowing that this might be the last time she would ever lay her eyes on the one whom she treasured above all others, she gave all she had to prepare him for burial by taking a vial of costly perfume and anointing his head. The others were indignant, deeming it to be a wasteful gesture. By contrast, God's opinion is clear.

If I speak with the tongues of men and angels... if I have the gift of prophecy, and know all mysteries and all knowledge... if I give all my possessions to feed the poor, and if I surrender my body to be burned, but do not have love, it profits me nothing. (1 Corinthians 13:1–3)

In Luke 10:42, Jesus told Martha that "only one thing is necessary." What is that one thing?

In Psalm 27:4, another great king, who was said to be a man after God's own heart, said to the King of kings, *"One thing* I have asked from the Lord, that I shall seek: that I may dwell in the house of the Lord all the days of my life, to *behold the beauty of the Lord* and to meditate in His temple."* (Or, as *The Message* puts it, "I'm asking God for one thing, only one thing: to live with him in his house my whole life long. I'll contemplate his beauty; I'll study at his feet.")

The one thing that is necessary is to sit at the feet of Jesus and take your place as a receiver. It is to behold his beauty. It is to spend time in his presence, admiring him, adoring him, and loving him, taking in all that he is and all that he has to give. It is to allow him the place he has always wanted to have in your life—to allow him to be the source and giver of all things.

The "one thing" is to be his Shulammite.

"No, read some verses from the Song of Songs, this other thing is of no use to me."

ST. JOHN OF THE CROSS, SIXTEENTH CENTURY,
having refused last rites from the friars on his deathbed.
When they finished reading, he exclaimed,
"Oh, what precious pearls."

Leaning

SONG OF SONGS, CHAPTER 8

"Who is this coming up from the wilderness
Leaning on her beloved?"

SONG OF SONGS 8:5

I had given considerable thought to another trip that I wanted to make with the queen. The kingdom was running fairly smoothly, so I determined that now was a good time to get away. As we sat together after an evening meal, I decided that this was an appropriate occasion on which to unfold my plans.

"We have known love on the mountaintops recently, my darling," I said to my queen, "but on the other side of every mountaintop there is a valley."

"What are you trying to tell me, my beloved?" she asked.

"I have been thinking. It is time, once more, for you to visit the wilderness," I said.

"Really?" she responded, her voice meek but reluctant.

"Yes. Only this time, I will be going with you."

"For what purpose?" she inquired.

"I would have to tell you a story to answer that," I said.

She smiled. "Then tell it, my king."

"About five hundred years ago, a wilderness icon surfaced from the desert. His name was Moses. Having fled Egypt, he left everything behind and spent forty years shepherding sheep in a no-man's land. Drained of all self-confidence, he emerged from the wilderness leaning on God and prepared to lead three million of our ancestors out of slavery to the Promised Land. As a consequence of Moses's wilderness experience, he gained a reputation as the most humble man on the face of the earth. Humility and being completely dependent on God go hand in hand. Humble people know who God is and who they are; who can do all things and who can do nothing. I will take you with me, and we will retrace Moses's footsteps."

"I will go with you, Solomon," she said, "but tell me more about what Moses, the man of God, learned in the wilderness."

"He learned to lean," was my answer.

"A strange reply," she responded. "Do you remember the time when I thought I had lost your love, and I sought you in the streets? When I found you, I clung to you as if I would never let you go. Do you think Moses was a 'clinger' or a 'leaner?'"

"Clinging is good, my dear, but leaning is far better," I answered with a smile. "You see, when Moses emerged from the wilderness, he was leaning on his staff, which became the rod of God. Through that rod, God's presence was manifest, and he demonstrated his authority and power. Leaning in complete trust is always better than desperately clinging. Moses knew how to let God be God."

Reclining, I continued with my story. "God picked this man to lead his people to freedom, but Satan, the adversary, issued a challenge. He wanted to keep our people in slavery under Pharaoh's domain. The result was an epic battle. The battleground was Moses's heart. From unseen realms, the Prince of Darkness offered Moses the world. But the living God offered Moses himself."

"I am intrigued," the queen said, her curiosity evident. "Tell me more. And what do you mean by 'the world'?"

I waved my hand as I spoke, taking in the room and the remnants of the meal before us. "The world is not just this physical space that we occupy. There is a spiritual dimension to it as well. It is made up of the lust that is in our flesh, the lust of the eyes, and the insidious pride of life, which has its end result in total self-reliance and disregard for God."

I leaned forward again, gazing intently into her eyes. "Growing up in Pharaoh's palace, Moses had any pleasure at his fingertips—any woman, any drink, any drug, any perverted pleasure. It was all his if he wanted it, but Moses said, 'No.' Instead, he chose to associate with the people of God and suffer ill-treatment with them. Because he did so, the first skirmish for Moses's heart belonged to God."

"I know the tale," she said, "but I have never heard it told in such a way."

"Then, in the story of the Exodus, we read that Pharaoh forced the Hebrews to build two entire cities, Pithom and Raamses, to contain all of Egypt's treasures. You can only begin to imagine how much treasure there was—the gold, the silver, the many jewels, the ivory, the other things of value. But the lust of the eyes, the pursuit of wealth, and the accumulation of things can all compete for the heart of a man and vie for his devotion. This was Moses's second test."

Her eyes roved the room with its high ceiling and gilded decoration. "Are we not also in danger, then?" she asked.

I smiled at her perceptiveness. "Although you have seen great riches, my love, it is not so much riches themselves that enslave a man or a woman—it is their call. Every day they call out, 'Give me your time, give me your sweat, and give me your life. Work harder, work longer, and you can own some paltry part of the glitter and the glamour of this world.' Moses grew up in Pharaoh's house—perhaps he could have become the next Pharaoh himself! But he abandoned all the treasures of Egypt in pursuit of a greater treasure: knowing the living God. By this, God could claim victory in the next round of this battle for Moses's heart.

"As a prince in Egypt's royal house, the heir apparent to Egypt's throne, Moses was also allotted every privilege. He ate the finest foods, dressed in luxurious clothes, and had the best education that Egypt had to offer. He, too, slept on a bed of ivory. He was honored as only royalty is honored. He was the envy of every citizen and slave. Such an upbringing could indeed make one proud. Yet, Moses refused to be called the son of Pharaoh's daughter. This added the finishing blow to the spiritual battle for who would lay claim to his heart. As a result of these conquests, and of forty years spent in the wilderness, Moses became the champion of humility."

I leaned forward again. "You see, my dear, God took Moses out of the world. Then, in the furnace of the wilderness, he taught him many lessons that would help him lead our people through the desert into the Promised Land. There in the desert, God took what was left of the world out of Moses. Finally, when God knew that the world would have no sway over him anymore, he sent him back to those held captive in the world so that he could be their deliverer."

"Might we too leave the world, my king?" she asked.

"One cannot successfully leave the world through his or her own resolve, duty, or sense of religious obligation. Love for God is the only acceptable motive, and that love comes from seeing him."

"What are some of the things you wish for me to experience in the wilderness, my love?" she asked. "Like Moses, I have a desire to be delivered from these enemies as well."

"We will begin where Moses began," I said. "We will discover the life and ways of the nomadic people who call the desert their home. We will learn of the warmth of their hospitality toward strangers; their ability to find water from rocks in dry, barren places; how to make bitter water sweet; and how they care for their flocks. We will also see where our ancestors' bodies fell in the wilderness due to their unbelief. We will walk where Moses walked and discover the spiritual lessons that God taught to one of his greatest servants."

"I am ready to go, my beloved, as long as you are with me," she told me emphatically.

Over the next few weeks, we prepared for our journey. We packed only a few small bags of clothes, along with some other belongings, and set out for the wilderness on the backs of camels, flanked by two dozen mounted guards. I left instructions with my trusted commanders about managing the affairs of the kingdom in my absence.

We journeyed some fifty miles west to the sea. From there, we were taken on the royal barge to Egypt. It had been many centuries since the Jews had been slaves in that land—but Egypt had not lost its beauty nor its attraction.

I had sent a message to Pharaoh telling of our visit. We were greeted as royalty is greeted, but I was quick to tell him that our reason for coming was private, not a state visit. I requested the privilege of fulfilling my purpose, which was to take my bride through some of the places where God's people had once been enslaved.

After a brief tour of Egypt, we were ready to set out together for the wilderness. Nearby, we could see the pyramids and the Great Sphinx. I looked around in all directions and then pointed east. "There is a desert out there," I told the queen. "It is a wilderness. It is mostly sand, heat, and pitiful shrubs, and it contains little water. It is from this place that our forefathers walked out of this land and moved eastward and then north to the land God had promised… the very land in which you and I live today."

I took a deep breath. My next words surprised her.

"There must be a wilderness in every person's life if we are ever to truly get to know God. It is not in our comforts, but in our lack of them, that we are pressed to discover who he really is."

Then came the fire in my voice, fire that I knew shone in my eyes. "But there is something far deeper than that. There is a wilderness with God! Without knowing that wilderness, we can never really know him. He is not there at our beck and call as the dispenser of riches and all good things. Many feel that is all that God is—a benevolent deity who gives us the wealth of life. But our God has built into him a wilderness that he dispenses to the children he loves. History records that the man of God, Moses, saw God not in palaces, but in a hot, burning desert when there was nothing around but gnarled shrubs and withered bushes. Tell me, my beautiful, wonderful wife, would you still like to retrace his journey through the wilderness?"

Knowing immediately that my question had a double meaning, she responded with a nod—and a duplicity of her own. "Yes, my king. I am ready for the Lord of my life to lead me anywhere he chooses, if it means that I will come to know him better."

So it was that we left Egypt with its glitter, fabled riches, and lying promises, and stepped out into the wilderness.

We began by visiting the famed oasis where Moses turned the bitter waters sweet. We met a desert tribe and spent several nights sitting around campfires with them. They made their home our home. Without knowing who we were, they treated us as if we were a king and a queen. We experienced God's provision one day at a time, and, in the midst of the scorching heat and desolation, drank from the hidden streams of the One who caused water to gush from the rock.

We were gone for several months before we finally returned to Jerusalem, rejuvenated by our adventures. This desert experience had a deep and lasting impact on both of us, but especially on my Shulammite. Like Moses, she had been changed.

When we arrived back in Jerusalem, my queen informed me of her strong desire to see my mother, Queen Bathsheba. "I would like to share with her all the things I learned in the desert," she told me. So the following week, we paid a visit.

We were transported to my mother's home in my royal palanquin. We arrived unannounced, wanting to make our visit a surprise. My mother knew that we had been gone, and she was anxiously awaiting our return. We stepped down, strolled up the stone walkway, and knocked on her door. A servant answered. Recognizing us, he raced off to retrieve Queen Bathsheba. When she saw us, she clapped her hands together. She was still beautiful in her old age. Her eyes lit up. "I am thrilled to see you!" she exclaimed.

Looking at the two of us standing in the doorway, she instantly perceived that something about my bride seemed different. She stared at her momentarily.

"Your manner and disposition have somehow changed," the queen said, with a quizzical expression. "You seem so... so relaxed. But I cannot put my finger, exactly, on what is different."

Hoping to discover the answer, she asked, "Tell me, my daughter, what it is? Please satisfy my curiosity. Who is this coming up from the wilderness leaning on her beloved?"

POINTS TO CONSIDER

The first time Solomon's bride came up from the wilderness, she emerged with a pleasing, fragrant aroma. The second time, she was calmly and confidently leaning on her beloved.

Trust in the Lord with all your heart and do not lean on your own understanding. (Proverbs 3:5)

By the time Solomon's darling came up from the wilderness the second time, the lust of the eyes, the lust of the flesh, and the pride of life had no grip on her. They held no attraction and were no threat to luring her heart away from her beloved.

Love for the world stands in direct opposition to love for the Father. Where did Moses find the strength to overcome these world forces? Hebrews 11:27 gives us the secret. It says that Moses "endured, as seeing [continually seeing] Him who is unseen." There is only one force in the universe able to disarm the powerful pull of this world and render it inoperative. That power inhabits the unseen. Seeing *him* makes all that the world has to offer seem a mere pittance.

Satan made the same proposition to Jesus in the wilderness:

And he led Him up and showed Him all the kingdoms of the world in a moment of time. And the devil said to Him, "I will give You all this domain and its glory; for it has been handed over to me, and I give it to whomever I wish. Therefore if You worship before me, it shall all be Yours."

Jesus answered him, "It is written, 'You shall worship the Lord your God and serve Him only.'" (Luke 4:6–8)

Moses left everything. James and John left their nets—their trade, their business, and their "world"—to follow Jesus. Paul left everything in his previous life and considered all he could have boasted about to be dung in light of knowing Christ. Jesus himself, who would never ask anything of us that he has not first done, left heaven to come to this fallen planet and dwell among sinful men. This is part of our calling: to be willing to leave all, in order to gain him.

THOUGHTS/PRAYERS

Is there anything of the world that still occupies a portion of your heart? Then give it to him. He is a jealous God. He wants it all so that he can become your *all*.

The same battle that was fought over Moses's heart is fought over the heart of every believer. The angels are watching. Whom will *you* love? Whom will *you* worship?

Do not love the world nor the things in the world. If anyone loves the world, the love of the Father is not in him. For all that is in the world, the lust of the flesh and the lust of the eyes and the boastful pride of life, is not from the Father, but is from the world. (1 John 2:15–16)

Lord Jesus, I know that this world has its pull. Deliver me from the trap of this world system, a trap which the enemy has laid in order to rob me of knowing all the riches that are in you. All that this world has to offer is nothing compared to knowing you. Deliver me, as you delivered Moses, by letting me see you—the one who inhabits the unseen.

Day Twenty-seven

The Unquenchable Fire of Love

SONG OF SONGS, CHAPTER 8

"Put me like a seal over your heart,
   Like a seal on your arm
For love is as strong as death,
Jealousy is as severe as Sheol;
   Its flashes are flashes of fire,
   The very flame of the Lord.
Many waters cannot quench love,
   Nor will rivers overflow it;
If a man were to give all the riches of his house for love,
   It would be utterly despised."

SONG OF SONGS 8:6–7

For days, a blustery, wintry rain pelted the mountains of Zion, delaying Solomon's departure to Jericho. At last, however, the clouds broke and the temperatures lifted, giving way to the warmth of the sun.

"Tomorrow, I must leave on my journey," said Solomon. He was looking forward to this trip to one of his favorite spots, particularly to bathing once again at the lush spring and oasis at Jericho. "Come with me as far as the summit of the Mount of Olives, and let us seize this opportunity to be outdoors. We can enjoy a meal together as we take in the beauty of Jerusalem and the surrounding mountains."

I was eager to join him and readily consented.

The following day, the two of us left the palace and made the mile-and-a-half trek uphill by foot, accompanied by the king's royal escort. We stopped near the mountain's crest and spread out a blanket. There, we shared a simple meal together while soaking up the view, breathing in the freshness of the air, and enjoying light-hearted conversation.

When we had lingered for an hour or two, the king said to me, "I must leave you now. My guards will escort you back to the palace."

"That is not necessary, my beloved," I said. "It is a beautiful day, and I prefer to walk. I will be all right. Do not worry about me." His face creased with concern, and I laughed at the worry there. "I was not always a queen, you know," I said. "I am able to walk on my own without fear. Besides, your servants are always near." My voice softened but lost none of its confidence as I declined his offer. "All I ask of you is this: put me like a seal over your heart and like a seal upon your arm while you are gone."

"You know that I will, my darling. My heart will not beat a solitary beat without being reminded of you, and like a seal upon my arm for all to see, there will be no doubt that I have but one love in my life, and that is you," he said softly, and he kissed me good-bye.

One of the royal guards handed him the reins to his steed. The king mounted and then rode off with his squad of soldiers. Stopping at the mountain's summit, he turned, waved to me, and then disappeared over the hill.

I began my descent down the mountain on the winding path that led to the city. Joy filled my heart. A smile graced my face. My thoughts were of the king. *I am married to a poet. He has such a way with words.* Occasionally, I even burst out with a giggle as I walked along, recalling some of his more amusing anecdotes.

As I approached the city, my concentration was suddenly broken by the sound of a crowd coming in my direction. I looked up to see what it was. Quickly, I realized that this was a funeral procession. They were on their way to the cemetery located outside the city on the eastern slope of the mountain. The wailing and crying grew louder and louder until the mourners got so close that I was forced to step off the path to let them go by.

As they passed, my eyes fixed on the corpse. It was wrapped in linen and was being carried on a litter by four strong men. My thoughts of joy were overtaken by grief as I felt the pain and loss of the family and loved ones who would never see this departed soul again.

Stopping one of the stragglers, I inquired, "Who was this person, and how was his life taken?"

I learned that it was a young man from a peasant background. He had been walking along in the Kidron Valley when, without warning, he was engulfed in the raging torrents of a flash flood that had coursed through the valley as a result of the heavy rains.

The procession continued its march toward the graveyard. I turned and resumed my way back to the palace. For several minutes, I brooded over the unexpected encounter with death that had interrupted an otherwise delightful day. Finally I gave up, sensing the futility of the human mind to understand or solve one of life's deepest riddles. Gradually, my peace and joy returned to me as my thoughts drifted back to the king.

The greatness of Solomon's love seemed to me almost as deep a riddle as that of death. I had long since abandoned the notion that my grip, weak as it was, could ever shackle the powerful force of his love. His love would always be there. It was freely given. It could not be purchased. It was constant, unchanging, unrelenting. It did not depend on my love for him. Like a blazing light, it continued to draw me toward him, eliciting in return more and more love from me.

Suddenly a new thought pierced my mind, and I gasped as if I were catching a glimpse into eternity. "Surely my beloved's love for me must be divine, planted in his breast by God himself. It is as the flame of God! This love is eternal, and by no means could it ever be extinguished. It will never fail. It is as strong as death! Once death lays hold of one of its captives, that one becomes death's prisoner forever and is never released. So it is with my beloved's love for me! I have become his willing prisoner of love, and he will never release me!"

By this time I found myself almost racing to the bridge which spanned the Kidron Valley and led to the city. My heart beat rapidly. Looking down from the bridge, I saw the receding waters which, days before, had taken the life of the young man who was now being carried to his burial. Then came a second, powerful revelation:

Many waters cannot quench love. Nor will rivers overflow it.

"Yes, it is true!" I cried aloud. "Many waters cannot put out the fires of this divine love. Nor can it be covered up forever—it is even as the rocks in the valley below. Eventually, the waters will recede, and we will see what was always there! Love must burst forth!"

Exhausted, I reached the gates of the palace.

Stepping back momentarily, I paused and looked through the gates at the magnificent structure. It had taken thirteen years to build. It was made of large, costly stones and the finest cedars from Lebanon, and it had been crafted by the hands of laborers, transporters, hewers, deputies, and overseers numbering thousands upon ten thousands. Then, like a hewer's hammer crashing upon stone, a third revelation was chiseled into my heart.

"This palace, the riches, everything—all are like a vapor. They are but naught compared to love. Let them all be utterly despised. There is only one prize, one quest, one thing alone worth living for. Let me live to know that which is eternal. Let me live to know his love!"

By this point in the Song, we see a woman who has truly grown in her knowledge of love. The Shulammite has become a secure woman. She rests in the sanctuary and confidence of Solomon's love. She has no fear or doubt in his love. And she recognizes that his love is a divine love, set on fire by the very flame of God. To borrow from the apostle John's commentary on the love of God in 1 John 4:16, she has not only come to know but to *believe* the love which Solomon has for her.

The Shulammite has also discovered that just as death is so dominant that it has never released its hold on one of its captives, so is love!

Not only was Solomon's love as strong as death, it was a jealous love. God had given Solomon vast "riches and wealth and honor, such as none of the kings who were before has possessed nor those who will come after" (2 Chronicles 1:12). Yet, he was jealous over one very small thing. He was jealous over the heart of a woman.

This too is only a picture of God's jealousy over us. Divine jealousy, like an unquenchable fire, stands at the door of our hearts waiting to consume all rivals. This strong, jealous, unquenchable love is at the core of God's very being. It burns as a passionate, unquenchable flame.

"Many waters cannot quench love, nor will rivers overflow it." Neither trials nor tribulations can separate us from God's love.

> Who will separate us from the love of Christ? Will tribulation, or distress, or persecution, or famine, or nakedness, or peril, or sword? Just as it is written, "For Your sake we are being put to death all day long; we were considered as sheep to be slaughtered." But in all these things we overwhelmingly conquer through Him who loved us. For I am convinced that neither death, nor life, nor angels, nor principalities, nor things present, nor things to come, nor powers, nor height, nor depth, nor any other created thing, will be able to separate us from the love of God, which is in Christ Jesus our Lord. (Romans 8:35–39)

Song of Songs 8:7 proclaims, "If a man were to give all the riches of his house for love, it would be utterly despised." We cannot buy this love or barter for it. It cannot be earned. It was God's free gift to us, and it became ours when he became ours.

So many mortals have tried to describe in word, song, poem, or prayer the love of God. Frederick Lehman captured but a flicker of its unquenchable fire in a song he wrote after the turn of the twentieth century, entitled "The Love of God":

The love of God is greater far
Than tongue or pen can ever tell;
It goes beyond the highest star,
And reaches to the lowest hell;
The guilty pair, bowed down with care,
God gave His Son to win;
His erring child He reconciled,
And pardoned from his sin.

O love of God, how rich and pure!
How measureless and strong!
It shall forevermore endure
The saints' and angels' song.

Could we with ink the ocean fill,
And were the skies of parchment made,
Were every stalk on earth a quill,
And every man a scribe by trade,
To write the love of God above,
Would drain the ocean dry.
Nor could the scroll contain the whole
Though stretched from sky to sky.

Selah. (Hebrew for "ponder this; meditate on these things.")
Lord, keep me in the grasp of your love, which is as strong as death and from which I never want to escape! Let your jealousy protect my heart and consume all rival loves. Thank you, Lord, for the trials that I am facing. Use them to prove that there is nothing that can separate me from your love. I choose to believe that this is the kind of love that you have for me. Make my tongue the pen of a ready writer to tell of your surpassing love. Help me to write a unique chapter in the fathomless story of your love.

"I see clearly that it is owning to our having too little practice in the love of God, which makes us think a soul cannot speak with God in such expressions."

St. Teresa of Avila, sixteenth century, on the Song of Songs

Our Little Sister

SONG OF SONGS, CHAPTER 8

"We have a little sister,
And she has no breasts;
What shall we do for our sister
On the day when she is spoken for?
If she is a wall,
We will build on her a battlement of silver;
But if she is a door,
We will barricade her with planks of cedar.
I was a wall, and my breasts were like towers;
Then I became in his eyes as one who finds peace."

SONG OF SONGS 8:8–10

While the king was still away, I received an unexpected message from my mother. The letter was brief. It read, "I must come to Jerusalem. There is an urgent matter I must discuss with you."

I immediately ordered an escort to leave Jerusalem, go to my mother's home, and bring her safely to the palace.

The following evening, one of the servants announced her arrival. I ran to the door to greet her and smiled to see her aging, familiar face. We embraced one another and traded kisses on the cheeks.

But Mother was not alone. Beside her was a thin, poorly clad girl of about twelve years.

Wrapping her arm around the young girl's shoulder, she said, "This is the daughter of Abigail and Erez, two of my dearest friends. She comes from our village."

I knelt down beside the girl and grasped her hand. "What is your name?" I asked, trying to look into her luminous brown eyes.

The young girl looked down. There was no answer.

"Mother, what has happened?" I asked.

"The child's father and mother were trapped in a fire that burned their home to the ground. Somehow, the girl was able to escape. I have no idea how she survived. She is now an orphan. She has no relatives. No home. No place to go."

My heart was consumed with sorrow for the child. I reached out, cupped my hands around her cheeks, and planted a kiss on her forehead. She did not move, but neither did she pull away.

Looking back to my mother, I said to her, "Thank you for coming, Mother. I will talk with Solomon about her when he returns. The young girl, does she have any clothing, any mementos?"

"None," Mother replied.

I smiled. "Soon, she will have many. You can leave her with me."

I begged my mother to stay, but she insisted that she must return on the morrow. She preferred her familiar, simple life in the village, difficult but predictable as it was, to the opulence of the king's court and a lifestyle that overwhelmed her.

For the next several days, I devoted myself to the young girl. A bond quickly formed between us. Love was born in my heart for this child.

When Solomon returned, I greeted him warmly. "It is so good to have you back," I said.

"And it is good to be back," he replied. "Let me clean up and have a bite to eat. Then I will tell you some exciting news from my trip."

He returned about an hour later, and the two of us sat together at our usual table. A servant brought Solomon a glass of cold water, along with a plate of breads, cheeses, and fruits. I listened intently as he related all of his exploits. When he was finished, he asked me, "And you, my dear, how have you been? Has anything exciting happened here while I was away?"

"Well, as a matter of fact, something *has*," I replied. Then I related, in great detail, the story of the young girl whom my mother had brought to me.

"Where is the child now?" asked Solomon.

"I will fetch her," I replied.

Leaving him at the table, I returned momentarily and brought the young girl to Solomon. She was dressed in a beautiful red garment I had made for her from fine linen with traces of gold and silver. Her hair was neatly brushed. No longer appearing as a waif, she looked like one who belonged to the palace.

Standing beside me, the child clutched my hand almost frantically.

"This is Shirel," I said. The young girl nervously bowed.

A welcoming smile broke forth on the face of the king. He extended both hands. "Come, my child, and sit next to me. Tell me your story."

It was love at first sight for the king as well. A young orphan girl had just bonded with the ruler of all Israel.

When they had spoken for a short while, we dismissed the young girl to the care of one of the maidservants, and Solomon and I began a lengthy discussion. I spoke first, laying out the whole situation as I saw it.

"We have a little sister," I began. "You will notice that she has not yet blossomed. She has no breasts. She is immature. But I have come to love this young girl. I want her to grow up with us. I want her to marry a fine young man someday, and I want to prepare her for the day she is spoken for."

"Very well," said the king. "But how well do you know her? How do you propose to raise the child?"

I thought back to my years in the village, to my friends there, and my eyes twinkled. "There are basically two kinds of young girls, my lord," I said. "First, there are those who are walls. These are the girls who say no to everything. They are not overly interested in boys and will put up resistance to any improper advances. On the other hand, there are those who are like doors. These are girls who are open to anyone and anything. Anyone who wants to come to them, they will let in. They have difficulty saying no to any proposition.

"If the young girl is a wall," I continued, "we will help protect and defend her. We will build upon her a battlement of silver. If she is a door, we will barricade her with planks of cedar and guard her, making sure that she is not taken advantage of."

I could see that he was following me—and from the appreciation in his eyes, enjoyed my use of allegory. I was beginning to speak like him, as I was well aware! But I continued. "I was raised as a wall, my king. There were many young men in my village who looked longingly at me and who had plans and schemes to make me their own, but I wanted to keep myself pure. I wanted to save myself for the man God had picked out for me and settle for nothing less. Thank God, that man was you! I want to raise this young girl in the same way. I want us to be able to present her as a chaste virgin to the one who will become 'the beloved' in her life. It will take both your input and mine, but this is something we can do together."

"If one day another man can have the joy that you have given me, I will gladly make the investment," said the king. "The highest expression of love is not only to love and be loved by another, but to increase that circle of love to include others. You have brought this lovely young lady into our lives. You have made her your own. And now she is *our* own."

I was overjoyed!

Again, I found myself speaking in allegory, following the well-worn paths of his own words. "You have told me before that my breasts were like two fawns. But today, I would tell you that they are more than that. They have become like towers, dripping with milk. I have nourishment to give, not only to you, but to others like this child. I am ready to increase our circle of love.

"I was once a young girl who, like all girls who fall madly in love, could think only about the object of my love. And that was you. My friends were neglected; my responsibilities shirked. I was caught up in a world that consisted of just the two of us. And rightly it should have been. But now I have grown in love, my king.

"Although I know that you love me unconditionally, and I have grown to love you in the same way, that eternal, divine, uncreated love that is in the bosom of God—and now in your bosom and in mine—knows no boundaries. It can be faithfully and totally committed to one, while at the same time flowing out to others."

The king gazed at me and smiled. "I admire you. You bring me such satisfaction. Yes, this is something we will do together, my love. We will embrace this child. We will raise her together. And we will prepare her to one day meet her own king."

POINTS TO CONSIDER

Jesus was the God-man. Not only did he have a perfect love for the Father, but he also had a perfect love for the human race. He never stumbled in either.

> One of them, a lawyer, asked him a question, testing him. "Teacher, which is the great commandment in the Law?" And He said to him, "You shall love the Lord your God with all your heart, and with all your soul, and with all your mind. This is the great and foremost commandment. The second is like it, you shall love your neighbor as yourself. On these two commandments depend the whole Law and the Prophets." (Matthew 22:35–40)

The Shulammite had recently been overtaken with a glimpse into eternity. She had seen that this divine, eternal love which she had known was as strong as death. It would never release one of its prisoners, and she was its captive. When one is filled with the source of all love, that love will not manifest itself in a selfish way. That love will overflow its boundaries and pour out into the lives of others. This is what we see in the Shulammite and her attitude toward the little sister.

The Shulammite had reached a level of spiritual maturity where the life within the beloved and her own life had become completely intertwined. Her character had become his character. His purpose had become her purpose. The Shulammite was concerned about her little sister, and so was Solomon.

When she spoke, it was not to say "I" have a little sister, but "we" have a little sister. It was not to ask what shall "I" do for our sister, as if there was something she could have done apart from him. Neither was it what shall "you" do for her, as if it completely depended on him and there was no part for her.

In John 14:9, Jesus said, "He who has seen me has seen the Father." Jesus is the ultimate illustration of God manifest in flesh. He was a seed who promised that if he fell into the earth and died, he would rise again and bear much fruit. This fruit would be the replica of the original. He was the firstborn among many brothers and sisters.

The eternal purpose of the Godhead has always been to expand the circle of the divine family. God wants to extend the life, the fellowship, and the love shared within the divine community—Father, Son, and Spirit—to a redeemed human race.

We see in the Shulammite the mature fruit that came from the original seed— ripe, full, and at peace. She is now wholly prepared to give her life away to someone besides Solomon.

What is the evidence that one's love for God is genuine?

Here is an example from the New Testament. Following the crucifixion, at a seaside breakfast, the risen Jesus fed his disciples with bread and fish (John 21). Then he singled out Peter and asked him the same poignant question three times: "Simon, son of John, do you love Me?"

Peter's answers were weak. They lacked confidence. He had recently denied the Lord three times. He could no longer boast that he loved the Lord enough to be willing to die for him. He was a broken man.

In spite of that, Jesus told him, "Feed my lambs."

Knowing your past failures and weaknesses, if Jesus were to ask the same question of you that he did of Peter, how would you respond? You might not be able to rise to the occasion any more than Peter did; you might not be able to give the Lord the answer you expect he would like to hear. Your answer might be something like, "Yes, I like you, Lord. I like you a lot. But I don't know if I love you enough to be willing to die for you. In myself, I know that I don't love you with the perfect love with which you love me." That was Peter's response.

Finally, after being asked the same question for the third time, Peter was reduced to saying, "Lord, you know all things."

But Jesus wasn't waiting for the perfect answer. Although Peter was a failure, Jesus saw in him the divine seed. He knew that there was a life in Peter that would rise. When that life was full, Peter would be able to deliver.

THOUGHTS/PRAYERS

Dear brother, dear sister, you would not have gotten this far in this book if you did not love the Lord. The question is, where is the outlet for that love? Where is your "little sister"? Who are the lambs that the Lord would have you feed?

Listening for the Word of God

SONG OF SONGS, CHAPTER 8

"Solomon had a vineyard at Baal-hamon;
He entrusted the vineyard to caretakers
Each one was to bring a thousand shekels of silver for its fruit.
My very own vineyard is at my disposal;
The thousand shekels are for you, Solomon,
And two hundred are for those who take care of its fruit.
O you who sit in the gardens,
My companions are listening for your voice—
Let me hear it!"

SONG OF SONGS 8:11–13

The wealth of my husband, King Solomon, was beyond description. But of all his prized treasures, the one he valued perhaps most was his vast accumulation of vineyards, stretching from the borders of the wilderness that leads to Egypt all the way to the highest hills of Lebanon.

The king rented out these vineyards to caretakers who tended the vines, harvested the grapes, and then returned a thousand shekels of silver to Solomon, while keeping two hundred for their own labors.

It was not uncommon for Solomon to arrive unannounced at one of his vineyards and then call together all the caretakers to instruct them. He would teach them about all aspects of raising the grapes and producing wine, from the planting, dressing, and pruning of the vines to the crushing of the ripe fruit and the fermentation and preservation of the juices.

I would often accompany him on these journeys to the countryside. I would listen to the instruction he gave and marvel at his unfathomable wisdom. I was a quick learner. Soon I too was able to teach others about the secrets of cultivating the vine and producing the best wine.

One day, while we sat together on a hill which had a panoramic view overlooking one of the king's large vineyards, I said to my husband, "You have trusted me, my king, to do you good all the days of your life. This vineyard is one of those that you sent me to purchase. I considered many fields, but the ground here was fertile, the climate right, and this one was the best. I instructed the caretakers to care for the vines with the wisdom that I have learned from you. You have eaten from the choicest grapes of this vineyard and drunk of its wine."

"A beautiful vineyard, indeed, my darling," said the king, "You have done well. And the fruit of the vine from this place is among my favorites. But I would have you know this one thing: of all the vineyards that I prize, one stands out above all others. That is you, my darling. You are more precious than all of these."

"I too have one vineyard which means more to me than these miles of vines which stretch far beyond what the eye can see," I said. "It is the vineyard that holds my highest affection, and the one which I will observe the greatest detail to care for. My vineyard, my very own vineyard, is before me. It is you, Solomon! I will labor for this vineyard without pay for as long as I live. You owe me nothing. It is my joy to let you have everything. You may have the thousand shekels that you are owed, and you can keep the two hundred as well."

As he chuckled, his eyes bright with his gladness in me, I continued, "I do have some business matters that I would like to discuss with you concerning these caretakers, my king. I have come to know many of them and now consider them friends. I have listened to their problems. They have many needs, but also many creative ideas. I know their circumstances well. They would love to hear from you in person, but they know me as your spokesperson and ambassador. Speak to me, my beloved, and tell me all that you wish to say to them."

"You have, indeed, always been a good listener, my darling," he said. "You have made my words your own. I trust you to represent me. You are not only the most excellent wife, lover, and friend that a man could ask for, but you are an excellent business partner as well. You know me. You know my ways. And you know how I run the affairs of my kingdom. Go now, and speak to them yourself. Respond to them with what is on your heart, for your heart has become my heart. You have my blessing. Make their lives prosperous. Make their vineyards profitable. Bring glory to this realm that God has given to us to co-rule as his caretakers."

Baal-hamon means "Lord of a multitude."

There were those sitting in the gardens, her companions, who were also listening for Solomon's voice. But the Shulammite asked, *"Let me* hear it!" She wanted to hear his voice so that *she* could bring his word to her companions.

What is the Word of God? Instinctively, most would answer that it is the Bible, because that is how they have been trained to think. And that is partially true, for the Bible is the written Word of God. But that answer will not pass the test on the day when we leave this world and are ushered into the presence of God. There we will stand face-to-face with the *living* Word of God, who is none other than Jesus Christ himself.

God is a speaking God. The Bible begins with him speaking the world into existence. Throughout the Old Testament, he spoke to the prophets and to the people. He spoke to Adam, Noah, Abraham, Moses, Samuel, Nathan, David, Solomon, Elisha, Isaiah, Ezekiel, Joel, Hosea, Jonah, Micah, Haggai, Zechariah, Malachi, and others.

In John's gospel, Jesus is introduced as the "the Word, who was with God, who was God" (John 1:1) and "who became flesh and dwelt among us" (John 1:14). The speaking God took up residence in a human body in the person of his Son.

Truly, truly, I say to you, he who hears my words and believes him who sent me, has eternal life. (John 3:24)

It is the Spirit who gives life; the flesh profits nothing; the words I have spoken unto you are spirit and are life. (John 6:63)

God, after He spoke long ago to the fathers in the prophets in many portions and in many ways, in these last days has spoken to us in His Son, whom He appointed heir of all things, through whom also He made the world. (Hebrews 1:1–2)

Every species has a language by which it communicates. God is no different. He has his own language, and that language is *His Son*.

In the Book of Acts we are told that "The word of God kept on spreading" (Acts 6:7).

Now the apostles and the brethren who were throughout Judea heard that the Gentiles also had received the word of God. [That could not mean that they all had received Bibles, because Bibles had not yet been printed. More-over, most believers in the first century were illiterate and could not read!] But the word of the Lord continued to grow and to be multiplied. (Acts 12:24)

In Hebrews we read:

For the word of God is *living* and active and sharper than any two-edged sword, piercing as far as the division of soul and spirit, of both joints and marrow, and able to judge the thoughts and intentions of the heart. And there is no creature hidden from *his sight,* but all things are open and laid bare to *the eyes of him* with whom we have to do." (Hebrews 4:12, empha-sis mine)

In 1 John, it says,

I have written to you, young men, because you are strong, and the word of God abides in you. (1 John 2:14)

Finally, in Revelation,

And I saw heaven opened, and behold, a white horse, and *he* who sat on it is called faithful and true, and in righteousness *he* judges and wages war. *His eyes* are a flame of fire, and on *his* head are many diadems; and *he has a name written on him* which no one knows except himself. *He* is clothed with a robe dipped in blood, and *his name is called the Word of God.* (Revelation 19:11–13, emphasis mine)

The Word of God is Christ. Christ is the Word of God. He wants to commu-nicate. His words are in us. Not only do we have his divine nature—his peace, patience, kindness, longsuffering, joy, and presence—within us, but we have his words: his ever-present, speaking voice.

Behold, I stand at the door and knock; if anyone hears My voice and opens the door, I will come in to him and will dine with him, and he with Me. (Revelation 3:20)

In Song of Songs 8:13, we hear the Shulammite's voice: "O you who sit in the gardens, my companions are listening for your voice—let me hear it!" The Shulammite was a listener. Shulammites feed on the words of God.

When we are young, we listen to people speak and teach us the Word of God so that we can grow. But more and more, we need to learn to listen, in order to hear the Word of God for ourselves. Then, as we hear and respond to the Word of God, we have something of great value to pass on to others.

Finally, as we come into maturity, we find that one of the most important things we can do is to be still and listen for the Word of God. We need to hear his words, not only to grow, but in order to stay connected to the Vine—just to stay alive!

All who follow in the footsteps of the Shulammite are good listeners. They are attentive to the king's voice. They are eager to respond. And they are anxious to impart his words to others.

THOUGHTS/PRAYERS

Speak to me today, Lord Jesus. Let me hear your voice. I crave to sit at your table in intimate fellowship with you, feasting upon your words. I want to be responsive to your voice. Let it divide my soul from my spirit so that I will know your will and do it. Open my mouth to speak the words that I hear so that they will be a source of strength and encouragement to your people. Lord, may your word continue to grow and multiply through me.

Intercession

SONG OF SONGS, CHAPTER 8

"Hurry, my beloved,
And be like a gazelle or a young stag
On the mountains of spices."

SONG OF SONGS 8:14

After our visit to the vineyards, King Solomon returned to Jerusalem, but I stayed behind in the countryside. There was much I needed to do; many caretakers still to visit. But as I went about my business, a nagging feeling continued to grow stronger inside of me. It seemed as if a quiet but persistent voice within was beckoning for me to get away and spend time alone with God.

The next morning, I rose early. Taking a flask of water, I retreated to a rocky knoll where I could view both the mountains to the north and the valley to the south. I found a place with trees for shade and a fallen log on which to sit.

A gentle breeze stirred, lifting my long, black hair slightly from my shoulders. I breathed in the views, relaxing in the peace and calm of this outdoor sanctuary.

I had brought with me a leather-wrapped scroll in which I recorded my diary. It was one I had kept from the time I was a young girl in the village, before I had ever met the king.

As my eyes slowly perused its entries, I relived experience after experience. And as I did, I was able to trace, coursing throughout my life, a golden thread of faithfulness. "God, you are truly a good God," I breathed as a prayer, with a deep sense of contentment.

I had come almost to the end of the space on which to write. Looking at the blank space, I commented aloud, "Today is the day I will complete this part of my journal."

With that, I picked up my pen and began to record what was in my heart.

To my dear heavenly King,

I am writing this to you today with a very thankful heart. As I look back, I see a tale of love and goodness splashed all over the pages of my life. I would like to take this time to recount some of your many blessings and to offer you thanks, from the depths of my soul.

I want to, first, thank you for my dear husband, King Solomon. Thank you for the flame of love that you set on fire in his heart for me.

From the time I first met him, I could not help but respond. I yearned for him to kiss me with the kisses of his lips and draw me that I might run after him. You answered my heart's cry.

But you were also using him to show me your own tokens of affection and to draw me to yourself, my most wonderful Shepherd King. It was then that the line between those things which are earthly and those things which are heavenly began to blur. For indeed, in Solomon's kisses, I began to know your own kisses of love as well.

With his first kiss, I realized that he was not only a king, but he was *my* king. You opened to me his world and that of his kingdom. I visited his garden. I strolled in his palace. It was on that day that you began to reveal to me that your sovereignty had been loosed upon my life. You are truly the King above all kings.

But your kisses did not stop there. You kissed me over and over and over again, showering me with your tender affections. You kissed me on the day when I saw that although I was black like the tents of Kedar, I was also lovely in your sight as the curtains of Solomon's bedchamber. You saw me as white as snow, as pure as purity itself.

You kissed me again when I saw how distracted I had become and that I had not paid attention to the dreams you had put in my heart. Solomon did not seem to care. He loved me unconditionally, as did you, my God.

Again, you kissed me when you led me to the kind and gentle shepherds; then again, with the king's promise that he would make something beautiful for me—the necklace of shields. Not only did the king hang around my neck a necklace of shields, but they were a symbol, also, from you. You, the Almighty, have been my protection. Indeed, you have made my life a thing of beauty, far beyond anything that I could have dreamed.

I could go on and list your countless other kisses, such as the kiss of rest and union that you gave me with Solomon as we lay together in the meadow. You have fulfilled the foretaste of that kiss. Not only did you allow me to enter into the rest of his kingdom and become one with him, but now, my God, I can see that you had an even greater goal. You have caused me to rest in you and become one with you as well. By your grace, I have discovered my purpose in this life and know you to be the real source of my life and peace.

I thank you, my heavenly King, that you are free, like the gazelles. And I praise you for your infinite patience, even in times when I have chosen to be bound with self-inflicted chains that put a wall between us. I declare to you, and call on heaven to take note, that I thank you for all the seasons of life—from the difficult winter to the blossoming springtime. You have taught me, through it all, to maintain a thankful heart in both good times and in bad, because in the end, it all comes from your loving hand.

I thank you for your longsuffering; for bearing the weight of my burdens. I thank you for all the trials that you have sent my way—even the persecution at the hands of the watchmen. You have used it all for good in my life.

I want to thank you most of all for all the times you have used Solomon to express your own words of love, "How beautiful you are, my darling." I have heard those words a thousand times, but still cannot hear them enough. He has been your image, your ambassador in my life, and he has communicated to me your heart.

As I have been to him a private garden, so I will be eternally to you, your own exclusive garden. Thank you that your love is stronger than death and will never release me from its grip. Death will die before your love for me could ever be severed.

With such a full heart and so much to be thankful to you for, O heavenly King, I come to this point in my life. I thank you that you have recently blessed Solomon and me with our little sister. You know her well, for she is your child. You even count the hairs upon her head. I thank you, also, for all the companions and friends you have given me. You know all of their needs, their struggles, their hopes, and their dreams.

Remember, dear God, that I was once just like all of them: a poor village girl— just a wildflower, a rose of Sharon. But then you drew me by your love. You wrapped your cords of love around me and have been drawing me, with each passing day, closer to yourself. Now, precious God, I make this simple request:

Look at my little sister. Look at my companions and friends. They are waiting to hear your voice too. Kiss my little sister. Kiss my friends, just as you have kissed me. Draw them after you so that they too will run after you. Be swift like a gazelle or a young stag on the mountains of spices, and come bounding to them, just as you have come to me.

With love and eternal gratitude,
Your Shulammite

"Hurry, my beloved, and be like a gazelle or a young stag on the mountains of spices." Some think that this final entreaty represents a believer's fervent prayer for the Lord's speedy return. *Maranatha.* Come, Lord Jesus! That may be true, and if so, none could fault such an interpretation. But the context seems to suggest another meaning.

What was the Shulammite thinking about at this point?

- "What shall we do for our sister?"
- "My companions are listening for your voice."

Does this portray a woman who is anxious about Solomon's return? Or does her concern center around her little sister and her companions?

Earlier in the Song, when she cried out to Solomon, "Be like a gazelle," she wanted her beloved to come to her. But now she is not thinking about herself. She is thinking about others—the immature and her friends.

Jesus Christ has been crowned King of kings and Lord of lords. Now, he also sits at the right hand of God as our High Priest. Besides ruling the universe and upholding all things by his power, as High Priest, Jesus is also our Intercessor.

Intercessors are those who take the place of another or plead another's case. They appeal to God on another's behalf, especially for those who desperately need God's intervention.

There are countless examples in the Bible of those who were called to intercede on behalf of others. Some were even willing to give their own lives:

- Moses prayed for the Israelites and was willing to be blotted out of God's book if God would not forgive them of their sin (Exodus 32:32).
- When King David disobeyed God by taking a census, he was willing to be destroyed in order for God to stay his hand against Jerusalem (1 Chronicles 21:17).
- Isaiah prayed with King Hezekiah to save the nation from defeat and destruction at the hands of Assyria, and the armies were suddenly turned back (Isaiah 36–39).
- Paul wished that he could be accursed if it would mean that his brethren and kinsmen according to the flesh (Israel) would come to know the Lord (Romans 9:3).

As our Intercessor, when we are in trouble or have a need, our Lord Jesus is always there representing that need before the Father.

Is it any wonder, then, that as we come to the end of this song, we see the Shulammite picturing for the believer one who has taken on more and more the nature of an intercessor?

Having first become a woman for the world, she has now become one who intercedes for that world.

"Hurry, my beloved, and be like a gazelle or a young stag on the mountains of spices."

THOUGHTS/PRAYERS

This is where the Song of Songs ends. The Song begins with the maiden praying that her king would come to her and ends with a prayer that he would now come to others in the same way. May this be our prayer as well.

Be swift, Lord Jesus. Kiss those whom I love so that they will know you as I have known you. Kiss them with the kisses of your mouth so that they will run after you!

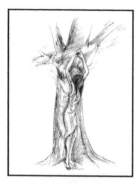

The Dreams

"…the mystery which has been hidden from the past ages and generations,
…has now been manifested
…which is Christ in you, the hope of glory!"

COLOSSIANS 1:26–27

I finished reading and slowly rolled up the scroll which King Solomon had given me, quietly securing it once again with the thin leather tie. The streams of tears that had flowed liberally from my eyes as I read had now begun to dry on my cheeks and glisten faintly in the candlelight. I looked up into the face of the king.

His eyes, too, were puffy and red. I could see the moist outline of tears traced upon his beard.

"My king," I said with a sigh, "I am emotionally spent. This song has plucked every string in my emotions. As I read, my feelings both soared to the heights and plummeted to the depths. It has hit upon a rainbow of notes, from longing and sadness to hope and bliss. Never has there been a song written such as this! Truly, this is for all of Israel to read. I came here today hoping to have the Shulammite revived and come to life once again in my memory and in my soul, but I received much more than I could have hoped or dreamed. Today, my king, I have encountered something sacred—something inspired—for no other song speaks of love as does this song."

"I have kept this song to myself until now," said the king, "but when I learned that I would see you today, I felt as if a voice within me was telling me that you must be the first with whom I would share it."

"You have honored and blessed me beyond that which I can express. If I could only but return the blessing to you in some way."

"You owe me nothing, dear Shirel," he said. "But, if you…"

"Excuse me for interrupting, my king," I said in a sudden burst of excitement, "but I think there is something that I could give back to you."

"What might that be, child?"

"Let me share with you one of my own memories. It came to me as I read the very last line of your song."

"By all means, speak freely," said the king.

"The song ends with a prayer. Indeed, the Shulammite was a woman of prayer. And I know that she prayed often for me. Let me share with you how those prayers have been answered.

"I remember one morning going to the garden together with the queen. As we approached the iron gate, she pulled a key from her dress and inserted it into the lock. The lock opened. She unbolted the gate, took a step back, and motioned to me to go ahead of her.

"Although you spent much time in the garden with her, it had become a favorite place for us to walk and talk together as well. We sat down on a bench under the shade of a well-groomed pomegranate tree, which had large, round fruits dangling in abundance from its branches.

"I was a young woman then, of sixteen or seventeen years. I remember distinctly the queen commenting on how beautiful, how mature I looked.

"Since being adopted by you and the queen, I had grown up in the palace and had observed, with great excitement, the construction of the glorious temple on Mount Moriah, just opposite from the palace on Mount Zion. I knew this was to be a house for the God of Israel. As the temple grew and neared completion, so did my desire to know this God of whom I had heard so much. I turned to the queen and was the first to speak, addressing she whom I now called 'mother.'

"'God has indeed answered your prayers for me,' I began. 'In the past two nights, God had been appearing to me, each night, in dreams. The first night, the dreams were very troubling; the second, very mysterious.' I asked her to help interpret these dreams for me.

"'Tell me, dear child,' the queen said as she grasped my hands in her own, 'What were these dreams? How has the God of Israel appeared to you?'

"'The first dream was terrifying,' I began. 'I was dreaming of a woman of unspeakable beauty who was being put to death on a tree. I shot up out of my bed, cold, full of fear, and shaking violently. For a long time, I simply sat there trying to make sense of the dream. I fought off sleep, wanting to be certain that I would not dream it again. When finally I yielded to the fatigue and to the darkness of the night, I returned to my sleep once more, only to be awakened shortly by a second dream.

"'This time, it was of a *man* who was being put to death upon a tree. As much as I struggled, the image held me. This man, this woman... I felt with great certainty that the man was somehow of royal birth, and the woman, incomparably beautiful, was his wife or perhaps his bride. The strange thing I noticed about this woman was that her face and her complexion seemed to change, as if she had ten thousand different faces, and her hair color with it—it started off as black as a raven, then turned to a strawberry red, then to a golden yellow, then to a deep, auburn brown, and finally to silver grays.

"'After what seemed like hours, I finally managed to return to sleep again, only to be awakened once more by a third dream. This time, the same image returned even more clearly, and I saw the couple not as two, but as one. She was being put to death with him. I was captivated with both terror and intrigue. I looked even closer. Then it appeared that she was not only dying with him—somehow, mystically, I saw them not as two but as one. She was not only dying with him, but *in* him. With that, the image vanished.'

"The queen gently wiped the sweat which had begun to ooze from the pours of my forehead. Remaining composed, she stared intensely into my eyes and inquired, 'Was there anything else? What were you feeling as you were beholding this scene?'

"'My emotions were undone,' I replied. 'I cried fiercely, uncontrollably. I could feel his love for her, and I could feel her passion for him. I wanted so much for them to live. I wanted to sleep again and dream this time a dream that they had not died, but had somehow survived. But such a dream forsook me. How could I make this dream change? How could it in some way have had a better outcome? I felt my soul crying out that a dream like this should not end this way. Everything in me rebelled at such a thought.'

"We sat in silence.

"'I will interpret this dream for you, Shirel,' the queen finally said in a soft voice. 'But first, you must tell me of the dream you received the following night, because I feel certain the two are related.'

"'The second night, again at about midnight, I was awakened by a dream,' I continued. 'This time, I saw the same young man again. His body had been taken from the tree, placed in the earth, and covered over with dirt. I could see his form lying beneath the ground, but housed within its ribcage, a small, pulsating, blue-white light was shining. My eyes were transfixed upon it. What it was, I did not know. I thought at first it might have been the young man's heart, but as I looked closer, I saw that it was not. It appeared connected to the man's heart, yet distinct. It actually had the form of a small seed.

"'As I gazed more intently at the light, it occurred to me that this light was alive. It was living, beating, throbbing, pulsating; and as it did, the brilliance from the light began to grow and the seed began to expand. Finally, a stalk burst forth from the seed, and the light began to rise from the corpse and slowly make its way to the earth's surface. It broke through the ground and then grew into a magnificent tree with all kinds of the most delectable fruits hanging from it. When I awakened from this dream, I was not troubled as before, only mystified. Yet, I was filled with an inexplicable hope that I could not quite grasp or understand.'

"'So, these are my dreams, mother,' I told the queen. 'What do you make of them?'

"Her eyes were streaming with tears as she listened to me finish the story of my second dream. 'What a glorious dream!' she exclaimed. 'Your dreams are indeed related, and the one cannot be understood without the other.'

"Then, she interpreted them for me.

"'Almost five centuries ago,' she began, 'our God appeared to Moses in a vision on the mountain in the Sinai wilderness. There, the heavens were opened to him, and he was given a revelation. God instructed him to construct a tabernacle on earth that was patterned after what he had seen in this heavenly vision.

"'Not long ago, our God appeared again to another of his servants, King David. He too was given a revelation. God gave him the plans to build the temple—even down to the last detail. Both the patriarch and the great king were instructed to build something on earth which would be a replica of that which exists in heavenly realms.

"'Here is the great secret—the great mystery—concerning that which they saw in the heavens. What they saw in the heavens was one and the same. *It was a man!* And he was the same man whom God has revealed to you!'

"'I am confused,' I remember bursting out in frustration. 'How could the tabernacle which Moses built and the temple which David was shown be patterns of a man who lives in the heavens? Does not God alone inhabit the heavens?'

"Then she replied, 'This is a great mystery—even a secret—which our God has kept to himself, with few exceptions, throughout the generations. But I can tell you, with all assurance, that it is so. Both men saw that somewhere outside of time and space, there is one who rules heaven and earth and sits on a throne ruling over all creation. But this same one is also the perfect sacrifice who will offer himself in order to restore this sinful human race to a relationship with the living God. It is a great mystery, indeed.'

"I asked the queen if you had spoken to her about this.

"'Not often,' was her reply. 'There are times when he will discuss this with me, but those times are rare. When he does, it is mostly with tears. For Solomon, this subject is holy ground.'"

The king clutched the arms of his chair as he sat listening, riveted to my story. "Did she say anything else? What else did she tell you?" he insisted.

"She told me about one time when you spoke to her about what you saw in that other realm. I could hardly believe what she told me. She said that she had been teasing you one afternoon about the extravagance of your throne and the manner in which royalty is approached—with all the foolishness and unnecessary drama. You became very pensive, almost withdrawn. Finally, you spoke.

"You said, 'I, like my father David, have had the curtain pulled back. I have looked into the heavenly realm as well.' You told her of your own gold and ivory throne, imposing, high, and lifted up. But you said that this throne was nothing in comparison. It paled in insignificance and caused you only shame when you considered what you saw when heaven was opened up for you. Because you saw *the throne*—the very throne of God!"

"Yes!" the king bellowed in anguish, no longer able to hold back. "I began to weep, and I fell to my knees. The queen dropped to her knees beside me and clung tightly to me with her arm around my shoulder. She tried to comfort me. Then I cried out—almost wailed—'I have seen the real king! He is my sovereign Lord. He is the sovereign Lord of every man who has ever held rule over others. I cannot express to you what that means. In every generation, in every age, in every nation, and of every tongue upon the earth are those who have been, those who are to come, all who have ever dared called themselves king... I saw the face and I saw the throne of the real King. I speak of the King of all kings and the Lord of all lords!'"

Amazed, I placed my hand over my mouth.

It took several minutes for Solomon's composure to return. He was crying once more—even convulsing. He continued trying to wipe the tears from his eyes with the sleeve of his garment.

"Forgive me," said the king, "for displaying such emotion. I will try not to interrupt like this again. Please continue. Tell me everything she told you."

"She continued to tell me of this one who inhabits the other realm. She compared him to the ark and the mercy seat which was made to inhabit the Holy of Holies in both the tabernacle and the temple and is guarded on the right and on the left by the imposing cherubim. This was only man's best, yet feeble, attempt to portray the reality of that which exists in heavens. As you yourself have now told me, she said that you not only saw that throne, but the One who sits upon it! That explains why the ark is made of wood—it represents a man, a perfect human—yet is overlaid and inlaid with pure gold, which represents divinity. Within that wooden, golden box are the tablets with the commandments, which speak of his perfect character; the rod of Aaron that budded, which speaks of his indestructible life that overcomes even death itself; and the pot of hidden manna, which speaks of the heavenly food with which he feeds the spirits of all humankind. This is the One you saw, is it not it, my king?"

His eyes seemed full of light as he answered, "Yes, this is the One I saw!"

His gaze urged me on, so I continued. "Then, the queen continued with the interpretation of my dream. 'I will now tell you how your first dream relates to the second,' she said. 'In the first dream you saw that a royal king died. That death was a sacrifice. You are also aware that when the high priest offers a spotless lamb as a sacrifice for the sins of the people on the Day of Atonement, he lays his hands on the head of the sacrifice, and thus symbolically identifies the sinner with the sacrifice. The two become one. The sins of the sinner are transferred onto the innocent lamb. This pictures the death of both—together. So it is with the couple in your dream.

"'The beautiful woman you saw represents the bride for whom this heavenly king was willing to die. Her many faces and the different colors of her hair show us that this bride, the eternal companion for the heavenly king, is made up not only of the sons and daughters of Israel, but of those he has chosen from all nations who have a passion and love for him.'

"Then, she came to the seed.

"She asked me if I remembered the story of the man and the woman in the garden of Eden—how they were placed between two trees, the Tree of the Knowledge of Good and Evil and the Tree of Life. She explained that when they ate from the one, something deep within them, which was created to access the heavenly realms, died. They never ate from the other tree—the Tree of Life—for if they had eaten, that divine life from the heavenly realm would have entered into them and they would have become new creatures—part earthly, part heavenly; part human, but part divine.

"She continued to explain that because of man's sin, God stationed the two fiercest creatures within his realm—two cherubim—in front of the Tree of Life with flaming swords of fire to keep the man and woman from eating and thereby living forever in their sinful state.

"It is not mere coincidence that, in the pattern Moses and David were shown for the tabernacle and the temple, there was a curtain hung between the Holy Place and the Holy of Holies, behind which the living God dwelt. On that curtain, Moses was instructed to embroider images of the cherubim. They still to this day are symbols of those living creatures in the heavens that guard the entrance to the presence of the glory of God so that no one can enter, save the high priest, and that but once a year.

"Then she told me that one day she had the hope that somehow, some way, that curtain would be removed and mankind would once again have the opportunity to enter behind the veil. God's purpose will not be deterred. He promised that he would defeat the enemy who brought on this fall. He will have what he purposed from before the dawn of time, and he will achieve it through the coming of a seed—*the seed of a woman!*

"I remember gasping and saying to her, 'Do you… do you mean to say that this God, this man—whatever he may be—who sits on the throne, will one day come to earth and take on human flesh?'

"'It is a mystery too great—even the greatest of all mysteries!' breathed the queen in a hush.

"'You have been shown, my dear younger sister, that this seed—who is the ultimate sacrifice—must die, and in his death we too will die. One day, he will come. One day he will go into the ground. And one day, he will doubtless rise again and grow up as a tree which will bear fruit like unto himself, in the very image of the original seed. That tree—the Tree of Life—will become available to the human race once again. That is the reason, Shirel, that something within you witnessed to the great hope you felt following the second dream.'

"Dazzled and stunned by such heady revelation, I slowly whispered, 'A divine seed, born of a woman, bearing fruit after its own kind… when will these things come to pass?'

"'No one knows for sure,' she replied. 'But in the fullness of time, he will come. Yes, in the fullness of time, he will come.'

"After that, a tranquil peace seemed to fill the garden and our minds as well, as we sat in silence. The time for words had ceased. I recall us both turning from each other and gazing at the inviting pomegranates that hung overhead, just within our reach. *Oh, the mysteries of the garden,* I remember thinking to myself. *No wonder Solomon loves to come here!*

"Now, I must ask a question of you, my king. Do you think that the reason this love song you have composed speaks so deeply to the heart is because it may in reality be describing not only one love affair, but two? Could it, in fact, be describing a love affair in two different realms at the same time?"

Solomon smiled, momentarily, with a look of deep satisfaction and contentment. His voice rumbled as he answered, "As the queen rightly said, it is a mystery. As surely as the dawn he will come, and in that day we will know."

"If you permit me, my king, I have but one last comment concerning your song."

"By all means, tell me what it is."

"Your song lacks a title—a name. As you know, the name by which I am called, *Shirel,* means 'song of the Lord.' I think that is a most appropriate name indeed, as I reflect upon the song of love that the Lord has been composing in my own life. But this song which you have written is like none other. Dare I say that if all of your other songs were to pass away, this one would ultimately endure? It is timeless. It touches the eternal. It has within it the breath of God. It therefore deserves a special title."

"And what would that title be?" inquired the king. "Do you have any suggestions?"

"Yes, I do," I replied. "It must be something simple, yet something profound. It must be something that sets it apart from all other songs, for truly this is the best of all your songs. I think that you should call it *The Song of Songs,* for that is what it is, and that is what it always shall be."

Acknowledgments

First and foremost, I have a profound sense of thankfulness to God for his love, his inspiration, and the precious times spent in his presence discovering the truths found in the Song of Songs. I also want to acknowledge Sandra, my wife and life companion for more than forty years, for her encouragement and the patience and endurance she displayed, day after day for a year-and-a-half, as I disappeared into our study to work on this project.

My deepest gratitude goes out to Betty Hawkins, Lori Drexler, and Donna Ferguson, who consistently prayed for me and for this book to make its way into print. To my "star" editor, Rachel Starr Thomson, and Jan Winterburn and Brenda Cox, who poured hours of time and energy into editing and proofreading, doing what I—in a million years—could never do. To the talented Tim Irvin for the artwork that has added such a touch of class to this book. To Gene Edwards for challenging me to become a better writer, for his gift of storytelling and desire and perseverance to try to impart a portion of that gift to me, and for having the audacity to suggest that I turn this into a "story"—a task which at first seemed light-years beyond any of my known abilities. Finally, to a group of Iranian house-church leaders who journeyed with me for five days, five to six hours a day, through the content of this book, weeping, worshiping, and receiving, whose lives were changed—as was mine.

Bickle, Mike. "Song of Songs: A Series of 24 Comprehensive Verse-by-Verse Teaching Sessions." Audio. Posted 2007. Mike Bickle's Online Teaching Library. www.mikebikle.org/resources/series/song-of-songs.

Driscoll, Mark. "The Peasant Princess." Audio. Posted 2008. Mars Hill Church. www.marshillchurch.org/media/the-peasant-princess/review.

Gill, John. An Exposition of the Book of Solomon's Song. Paris, AR: The Baptist Standard Bearer, 2002.

Glendhill, Tom. The Message of the Song of Songs. Downers Grove, IL: Inter-Varsity Press, 1994.

Guyon, Jeanne. The Song of Songs. Jacksonville, FL: Seedsowers Publishing, 1990.

Hicks, B.R. The Song of Love…From the Song of Solomon. Jeffersonville, IN: Christ Gospel Press, 1981.

Kaung, Stephen. God Has Spoken In…Job, Psalms, Proverbs, Ecclesiastes, Song of Songs. Richmond, VA: Christian Tape Ministry, 1990.

Kilpatrick, Martha. Adoration. Jacksonville, FL: Seedsowers Publishing, 1999.

Miller, Ed. "Song of Solomon." Audio. Posted 2004. Bible Study Ministries. http://www.biblestudyministriesinc.net/Song_of_Solomon.php.

Nee, Watchman. The Song of Songs. Anaheim, CA: Living Stream Ministry, 1993.

Nelson, Tommy. The Book of Romance. Nashville: Thomas Nelson, 1998.

Pope, Marvin H. Song of Songs. Garden City, NY: Doubleday, 1977.

The New Covenant

The Lord's Supper

Called to Rebuild

An Evening in Ephesus

What is the New Covenant? What is the relationship between the Old Covenant and the New? Are both covenants still in effect? Does God still have a covenant relationship with Israel? Are there still Bible prophecies waiting to be fulfilled concerning the modern state of Israel and the rebuilding of a temple in Jerusalem before the Second Coming of Christ? How did the New Testament come into being? How is the Lord's Supper to be celebrated, understood, and practiced? You will find answers to these questions and more in this New Testament trilogy featuring The Messenger, The Message, and The Marriage. In The New Covenant, Bible commentary, doctrine, the prophetic word, the saga of the first century church, and New Testament principles to live by all converge and come to life in this one, spellbinding story!

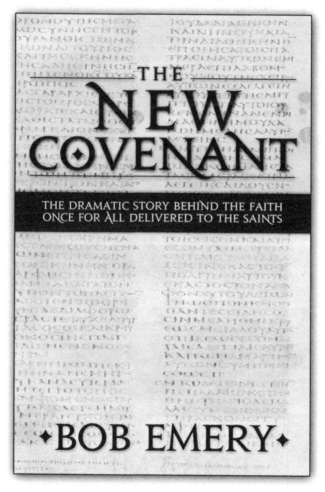

THE LORD'S SUPPER
THE CELEBRATION OF THE NEW COVENANT
(An excerpt from *The New Covenant,* published by BenchPress Publishing 2013)

The New Covenant (or New Testament) is more than a collection of writings consisting of the four gospels, the book of Acts, various epistles, and the book of Revelation glued and stitched together between a leather jacket. It should primarily be understood as the present, eternal, relational reality between God and his people. As we examine the overarching theme of the whole Bible we see that this relationship is a love relationship—a marriage relationship-- between Christ and his bride, the church. For many, the true meaning of the Lord's Supper has been virtually lost. Draping it in layers of institutionalism, superstition, and religious attitudes borrowed from pagan religion, the enemy has done a masterful job of robbing Christians of their true inheritance in understanding and celebrating the sacred and mysterious significance of this simple transaction that governs our relationship with our Creator and Redeemer. In The Lord's Supper, these layers are stripped away to reveal that each time we partake of the bread and the cup, our eternal union with our Lord is truly something to celebrate!

CALLED TO REBUILD
The Restoration of the House of God

A commentary on Ezra and Nehemiah, along with the other "remnant books" of the Old Testament—Haggai, Zechariah, and Malachi. *Called to Rebuild* examines these precious books and draws application for those who would be the spiritual descendants of that remnant in this generation. This book is for those who have a heart to rebuild and see the church of today become all that God intended for it to be.

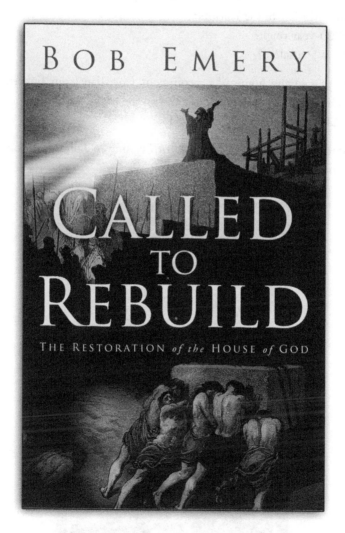

AN EVENING IN EPHESUS
With John, the Son of Zebedee
A Dramatic Commentary on the Book of Revelation

If you were a Christian in the first century and had received John's letter from Patmos, how would you have understood:
- The Beast?
- 666
- Babylon, Mother of the Harlots?
- The 1000-year reign?
- The New Jerusalem?

Join a meeting in the home of a prominent Christian from Ephesus, as the apostle John pays a visit following his exile on the Island of Patmos and explains THE REVELATION OF JESUS CHRIST!

(An updated and expanded version of *An Evening in Ephesus* is contained in part three of the trilogy *The New Covenant.*)

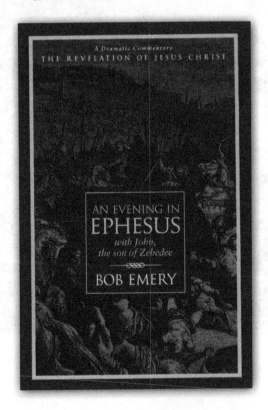

Made in the USA
Monee, IL
31 October 2023